7 Steps to Freedom

7 Steps to Freedom

A Systematic Guide to What Everyone Wants

GILBERT MANE

DELPHIAN BOOKS

Reprinted 2017
First published in Australia in 2009
by Delphian Books
(a division of New Frontier Creative Services Pty Ltd)
ABN 45 060 505 704
6 Merle Street, Epping NSW 2121, Australia
Tel: +61-2 9876 1050

©2009 Gilbert Mane

This book is copyright. Apart from any fair dealing for the purposes of private study, research, criticism or review, as permitted by the Copyright Act 1968, no part may be reproduced by any process without written permission. Enquiries should be addressed to the publisher.

All rights reserved.

National Library of Australia Cataloguing-in-Publication data:

Mane, Gilbert Simeon. 1955-.
7 steps to freedom, a systematic guide to what everyone wants

ISBN 9780977549160 (pbk.)

Includes index.
Bibliography.

Subjects: Self-actualisation (Psychology).
Self-esteem. Happiness. Success
158.1

Cover & Internal Design: Ronald Proft
Subediting & Indexing: Kristina Proft

DELPHIAN
BOOKS

www.delphianbooks.com.au

Where did you come from, baby dear?

Out of the Everywhere into here.

George MacDonald, 1824–1905
Poet, novelist, minister

To Leon MacLaren,

Teacher and Guide

And to

my wife Sarah,

Chief nourisher in life's feast

ACKNOWLEDGMENTS

I have received enormous encouragement and support in writing this book from every quarter, my many friends, tutors and fellow travellers in the School of Philosophy in Sydney chief amongst them; and for their love and support, not only in writing this book, but in several decades of work together I should like to offer humble thanks. I also have friends in many of the other branches of the worldwide family of the Schools of Philosophy to whom I am most grateful, but above all my deepest gratitude is to Leon MacLaren whose vision of truth and justice gave rise to these schools and to whom this book is in part dedicated.

Going back a bit further I would love to thank my parents Sam and Dawn and my brother David for giving me the best childhood and adolescence and adulthood I think anyone has a right to expect and for instilling in me that spirit of enquiry and curiosity which, I feel, have allowed me to jump from one stepping stone to another to get me where I am today.

More immediately several people have held me by the hand and helped me to produce the book you are now holding. Ron and Kristina Proft, publisher and editor (respectively) and my extremely good friends, have helped every step of the way; Ann Wakeford read the manuscript at an early stage and showed me how to adjust my writing to make it much more readable (and shorter); and Dexter Petley of the Oxford Editors offered wonderful advice.

And finally my deepest thanks to my wife Sarah who supports everything I do with loving encouragement and intelligent scrutiny – I certainly need both.

Everyone has contributed in some way to this book. They can take much of the credit for all the good bits. Any mistakes are mine alone.

Gilbert Mane
May 2009

DISCLAIMER
Although I have been enrolled as a keen student in the School of Philosophy in Sydney since 1975 and owe the vast majority of my experience of the work on self-awareness to that august institution, in writing this book I have not sought nor been given any formal permission or authority to speak on its behalf. Nothing in this book should be taken as any official pronouncement of the School nor do my views represent the views of the School. A similar disclaimer goes for all the other people, groups and organisations mentioned and quoted in these pages.

I encourage anyone who reads this book and finds their interest piqued by any of the organisations or people mentioned to make their own careful enquiries to find out if you want to go further with any of them.

Every effort has been made to trace and acknowledge copyright. However, should any infringement have occurred the publishers offer their apologies and ask copyright owners to contact them.

CONTENTS

Why You Should Read This Book

The Problem

Everyone wants to be free and happy. But many of us feel unhappy, constricted, confused and we seem to have little or no control over the external events which shape our lives. We may *try* to exert control over things and especially the people around us – our colleagues, children and spouses. We try to control external events. But this tight desire to make sure everything goes our way leads to stress, criticism, anxiety and even disease. We want happiness and freedom and they continually elude us. Just as life seems to be settling down to a comfortable, or at least predictable, pattern a metaphorical freight train comes out of the fog and sends us into a spin. Or, all too infrequently, a bunch of flowers and chocolates with a nice little note appears. We try to avoid the train wrecks, and to collect the bouquets. Our lives might be summarised as an unending pursuit of pleasant experiences, and an equally conscientious effort to avoid unpleasant and painful experiences.

Some of us are better at this than others, but in this pursuit external events have all of us enslaved. Life throws up constant challenges, disappointments, pitfalls and other stumbling blocks. We may be doing well at work, and then our spouse finds a chink in our emotional armour. Or we are finally sailing smoothly on the domestic sea, when someone runs into our car. Our house is finally where we want it, with every cornice painted and the plumbing working to perfection, and the boss needs us to work on our son's birthday. And we come to accept that life consists of these little ups and downs. But some of these ups and downs are not so little: the death of loved ones; horrible crimes; war and disease; political upheaval. These bring tidal waves of suffering to us or to others.

Our inner world

And we don't just have these external events to deal with. We have an inner world of thought, feeling and self-awareness to contend with as well. While saints and sages may speak of an inner Self which is conscious, full of knowledge and endlessly blissful, most of us find such a Self elusive, to say the least. *Our* inner self, like the external world, often seems anything but peaceful, calm, serene and detached from 'the thousand natural shocks that flesh is heir to.'[1] We are all too conscious of those dark, secret recesses of the heart and mind. These come in all shapes and sizes: anger, jealously, greed, guilty secrets, and a sort of dreary nostalgia which casts the present in a dull and discouraging light. There is criticism, irritation, judgment, requirements; or envy and resentment; anxiety, fear and an 'I-hope-it-never-happens-to-me' anticipation of the future – a sort of hopeless hope.

All this can lead us to wonder if unending freedom is even possible; we may come to believe that such freedom and happiness are unattainable; and many end up thinking that we are born, we are buffeted by life's events, and then, with a sigh of relief, we die.

But if, on the other hand, we believe that ultimate freedom is attainable and we wish to set out on a path to discover it for ourselves – we should be clear that it is freedom from our response to these external challenges and our inner negative reactions and tendencies that we are talking about. The question isn't so much: 'How can I be free of the boss's anger; my children's misbehaviour and my neighbour's loud parties?' It is rather, 'How can I be free of my knee-jerk reactions to these things?' The ultimate freedom is freedom from our own negative, limiting feelings and ideas which make us unhappy.

The state of the world

And when we turn from the condition of our individual lives to the state of the world what do we see? Alienation, anxiety; society in disarray and beset by fears – some well-founded, some illusory – about disease, drugs, war and the state of the environment; young people ceaselessly roaming

---

[1] William Shakespeare, *Hamlet,* act 3, scene 1.

the world looking for meaning and authenticity in their lives, the middle aged trapped in boredom and worry about financial and emotional meltdown, and the elderly either trying desperately to find the elixir of youth under the plastic surgeon's knife or going quietly to their final rest.

And our media present us with the daily obituaries – death here, war there, famine somewhere else. Good news is no news: a shark bite at a beach takes precedence over the fact that all across the world a vast and growing majority of children go to bed well fed; the sex-life of a pop singer is breathlessly reported while the incredible work of innovative schools in inner cities is ignored. In many ways the world has never been more peaceful and prosperous but survey after survey shows that many of us think we are living in times of danger and dislocation. We are paralysed by fear when few of us have anything substantial to actually be fearful of.

Questions

All of this existential angst motivates many of us to ask if there is more to life. Is life merely a journey from the maternity ward to the funeral home; from conception to cremation? Is our purpose simply to accumulate possessions and relationships and responsibilities until, weighed down by cares, we almost yearn for that final release?

And some of us ask: Who am I? Surely there is more to me than just a physical body with a bundle of reactive feelings on a hair-trigger. Perhaps, at last, we wonder if there is someone who can show us a way off this treadmill of unceasing labour for uncertain returns.

The Solution

My aim in this book is to set out some effective answers to these questions; to outline a practical method for attaining freedom and happiness; a method which is particularly suited to those of us who have family, work and social responsibilities. My heartfelt conviction is that those who read this book will benefit from it; and if we make the effort to find freedom for ourselves then those around us benefit as well. While I believe that there is more good to be found in the world than evil – more compassion than selfishness – more kindness than cruelty – we can always do with more of the good stuff. I believe the best way to ensure that the light outshines the darkness is for society to reach a tipping point where large numbers of men and women start to seek answers to existential questions about the meaning and purpose of their lives; to make the effort to raise their level of consciousness and awareness; and to take the necessary steps to achieve happiness and freedom for themselves and others.

My Background

I have always wanted to be free and happy. Through great good fortune I came across teachers and guides who showed me a way to go free, while still living a productive life in the society of friends, family, colleagues and fellow countrymen. This book is an attempt to present a system for those who, like me, are thirsting to discover an effective way to make fleeting happiness permanent, transitory wakefulness long-lasting and ephemeral knowledge solid and real.

It is my hope that some of the spiritual work and study I have done over more than thirty years can be synthesised for those who wish to set out on this adventure of the spirit. The idea of this book is to take one of the many paths expounded by the wise and give it a practical and informative shape, so that reasonably conscientious readers can begin to experience for themselves the freedom, fulfilment and empowerment which comes from tapping their inner source of wisdom.

In this book I deal with each of the seven steps to freedom, and recount anecdotes and illustrations for ease of understanding. Most importantly, at the end of each chapter I give a few practical exercises so that you can experience these steps for yourself. My advice is to read each chapter and either do the practices then, or read the whole book and go back and make yourself a program. The key here is to give the practices a go, and find out which of them 'speaks to you'. With all the practices suggested in this book, certain emotions are helpful: patience, fortitude, a spirit of adventure and enquiry – and sometimes a sense of humour. If you have tried self-improvement in the past, you will know that an earnest, heavy and serious approach can in itself be a daunting prospect, and an actual hindrance to progress. So let us take heart and begin on our journey to freedom and happiness.

I should like to wish all my readers the best of good fortune and all the freedom in the world.

* * * * * * *

Some Useful Information

Yoga Vasishtha

The seven steps to freedom were originally set out in the *Yoga Vasishtha*, which is one of the major works of Vedanta. This work consists of a conversation between Prince Rama and his guru Vasishtha, and it covers a vast range of spiritual wisdom. In Book III Vasishtha lays out these seven steps to wisdom, freedom and happiness, as follows:

> *I shall now describe to you, O Rama, the seven states or planes of wisdom. Knowing them you will not be caught in delusion:*
>
> *Pure wish or intention is the first;*
> *enquiry is the second;*
> *the third is when the mind becomes subtle;*
> *establishment in truth is the fourth;*
> *total freedom from attachment or bondage is the fifth;*
> *the sixth is cessation of objectivity;*
> *and the seventh is beyond all these.*[2]

Self-knowledge

Vasishtha says that the seven steps are states or planes of wisdom, and the highest wisdom is self-knowledge. Self-knowledge is the goal of the seven steps and is different from the mere gathering of information, no matter how useful. Until information is synthesised through experience, practice

---

[2] *Yoga Vasishtha* III.118.5–7.

and understanding, it is merely food for the chattering mind. Through experience and understanding information is transformed into knowledge and becomes part of our nature.

When we learn to drive, for example, our initial attempts are clumsy and a little haphazard until, after practice it becomes second nature. Similarly practice turns information about our inner self into the real experience of self-knowledge. This self-knowledge is the key to freedom and bliss. Understanding our true Self frees us from the illusion that we are a limited being, subject to the accidents of fate.

Take an analogy: Imagine you have been in a terrible accident and you are suffering from total amnesia. You lie there frustrated in your hospital bed and the doctor comes in, and tells you your name. It sounds completely unfamiliar. She shows you photographs of your family and friends and they mean nothing to you. But gradually, through the persistence of relatives, friends and your kindly doctor and her support team, a dawning light of memory begins to awaken and you can start to put the pieces back together. You begin to get a glimmer of who you really are. All going well your memory is eventually restored.

Waking Up

We have all been in that accident and we have all forgotten who we really are. We are all walking around in a dream existence. As Shakespeare says:

> *This is a strange repose, to be asleep with eyes wide open;*
> *Standing, speaking, moving, and yet so fast asleep.*[3]

But the Universe is gently and persistently trying to wake us up to the reality of who we are. Life is like a universal school, with a curriculum devised for our benefit, so that ultimately we can be free to rise to our true stature. Our teacher – life itself – keeps sending us lessons. We experience happiness and contentment when we learn the lesson, and suffer discomfort and pain when we turn our back on what we need to learn. This universal school is not haphazard and lawless and chaotic. It has rules and systems and natural processes. And one of the chief challenges

---

[3] William Shakespeare, *The Tempest,* act 2, scene 1.

of the human condition is to discover these fine regulations and, having discovered them, to make some effort to live by them. Part of the task of the wise through the ages is to reformulate these laws for the people and time in which they find themselves. Throughout this book I will be referring to the words and teachings of these great men and women who have expounded the rules of life.

FACT BOX   **The Bhagavad Gita**

This is a core religious text of Hinduism. It is a small part of the Mahabharata, the largest literary work in existence. The Gita's eighteen chapters contain the dialogue between the Prince Arjuna and the Lord Shri Krishna.

They are on a battlefield at the commencement of hostilities in a great war. How they came to be there is told in great detail in the preceding volumes of the Mahabharata and the course of the battle and its consequences are recounted in the following volumes. The Gita opens with the armies arrayed ready to fight. On one side are forces led by the wicked Duryodhana, including many of Arjuna's relatives and friends. On the other side are the forces of good, led by Arjuna's brother, the wise and honourable Yudhishthira. Krishna, Arjuna's cousin and friend, is his charioteer in the battle. Krishna is also the incarnation of the God Vishnu.

Arjuna has the task of initiating the battle by blowing his conch shell. So he asks Krishna to take his chariot out between the armies. He surveys the opposing forces and, seeing his friends and relatives whom he is duty bound to fight, he is unmanned by grief and despondency and throws down his weapons. He sinks to the floor of the chariot and turns to Lord Krishna and asks for his advice.

The Gita is the record of their conversation. Each of the eighteen chapters covers a major pillar of spiritual knowledge. It addresses, for example, the way of action, the way of devotion and the way of knowledge; it examines the issues of renunciation, relinquishment of the fruits of action, and the nature of consciousness.

The Gita has been a source of wisdom, study and consolation for millennia, and it has helped shape the outlook of a civilisation.

Seven

Why are there seven steps to freedom? Why does the number seven turn up so frequently in spiritual matters? One of the interesting aspects of universal rules is the role that certain numbers play. The number seven has importance and significance in all traditions.[4] Some say that seven reflects the natural order of things – a natural quarterly division of the twenty-eight day cycle of the moon; the seven-fold structure of certain constellations, the seven known 'planets' of the ancient world: Sun, Moon, Mercury, Venus, Mars, Neptune, Jupiter; the seven notes of the octave (returning to DO as the eighth). The number seven appears again and again in systems of cosmology and spiritual endeavour, and seems to have an innately satisfying sense of completion.

To take a few examples, we see in the Vedic tradition there are seven centres of energy in the body known as chakras: located at the base of the spine; the navel; the solar plexus; the heart; the throat; between the eyebrows; and the crown of the head. Each has a characteristic colour and set of attributes and, according to the system of yoga, the power of each is enlivened and becomes actively available to an individual through appropriate spiritual discipline.

In the *Bhagavad Gita* the Lord Shri Krishna lists seven attributes of a man of steady wisdom. The Parsees refer to seven immortal saints: good intentions; utmost fairness; the longed-for kingdom of God; pious modesty; perfect health; rejuvenated immortality; and watchful obedience. The Bible is full of references to the number seven. Jericho, the entry point into the Promised Land, is famously defeated when, according to the song, 'de walls came a'tumblin' down'. How was this extraordinary feat accomplished? Seven priests with seven rams' horns walked around the city for seven days. On the seventh day 'they compassed the city seven times' – the Israelites then gave a battle cry and the city walls came down.[5] This story is an analogy of the walls of our ego-based ignorance tumbling down in the face of the call of truth, and the number seven clearly plays a key role.

Jewish doctrine says there are seven qualities of God known as the seven Sefirot each of which is exemplified by one of the great patriarchal figures in the Bible (see Table 1).

The Book of Revelations, the last and in many ways the weirdest Book of the Bible, is full of references to the number seven: the revelation is addressed to the seven churches; the Lamb has seven eyes and seven horns; the dragon has seven heads; the wrath of God is pent up in seven vials; and the Book itself is sealed with seven seals.

---

[4] H Biedermann (J Hulbert, trans.) *Dictionary of Symbolism: Cultural Icons and the Meanings Behind Them,* Facts on File, New York, 1992, p. 302.

[5] Joshua 6:6–20.

TABLE 1: The Seven Sefirot

Sefirah	Characteristic	Patriarch
Chesed	Loving kindness	Abraham
Gevurah	Might, Judgment	Isaac
Tiferet	Beauty, Harmony	Jacob
Netzach	Triumph, Eternity	Moses
Hod	Majesty, Splendour	Aaron
Yesod	Foundation	Joseph
Malkhut	Kingship, Sovereignty	David

Seven levels of mankind

In Chapter One and at various points in this book I will look in detail at a model whereby the whole of mankind is divided into seven levels. There is an outer circle of three levels consisting of those governed by their appetites, those governed by faith and those governed by reason. And there is an inner circle also consisting of three levels of the great teachers and men and women of wisdom: prophets, gurus, founders of religions, master teachers and fully realised sages. There is little direct communication between the inner and the outer circles; they speak a different language, have different interests, motivations and goals.

> *The saint is awake when the world sleeps, and he ignores that for which the world lives.*[6]

The getting and spending, ambitions, triumphs and disasters of the outer circle have little or no significance for those in the inner circle. Similarly the inner circle, on those rare occasions when they make themselves known to the outer circle are ignored, shunned or, worse, attacked and sometimes killed. Their message is, to say the least, not generally well received.

But between the inner and outer circles there is a stage linking level three and five – which connects them. This fourth level, for reasons I will go into in Chapter Four, is not always occupied. The people at this level

---

[6] Shri Purohit Swami, *The Geeta,* Faber & Faber, London, 1973, p. 26.

hear the teachings of the inner circle. They also understand the outer circle. Their task is to translate the principles, doctrines and ideals of the wise into a system and language which the outer circle can hear and follow. It is one of the tasks of a school of human development to raise the level of consciousness of some to level four so they can hear and respond to higher wisdom and enact and proclaim it in such a way that ordinary people in the outer circle can follow.

The seven days of creation

One of the most famous 'sevens', of course, is the opening account in Genesis of the creation of the universe in seven days. There are many ways of looking at this story – as a great mythic account of the creation, as literal truth, as manipulative nonsense, as symbolic allegory. I prefer the last option so, in each chapter of this book, I will look at the subtle, symbolic meaning of each of the seven days of creation. I will examine each day to discover what advice and guidance the author of Genesis gives us on our journey along the seven steps to freedom.

It may seem odd to look to a text composed millennia ago in the Middle East by Hebrews, for guidance on a system set down in India at an indeterminate time in the past. My hope is that, as you read this book, you will see that each day relates to each step and that this in itself is a mysterious, thought-provoking phenomenon, raising questions about the single message that the wise of all races, religions and eras are here to deliver; and perhaps prompting some further enquiry into the fundamental unity of all scriptures and religions.

FACT BOX   **Gurdjieff**

Georgi Ivanovitch Gurdjieff (1866?–1949), a Russian of mixed Greek and Armenian parentage, was a teacher of esoteric wisdom which (he said) he gleaned from his travels and his meetings with remarkable men (the title of one of his books). These travels took him to Egypt, Europe and Central Asia in a quest for the source of universal wisdom.

He appeared in Moscow in 1912 and began to attract followers and students to his teaching. These included the journalist PD Ouspensky and the composer Thomas De Hartmann. During the upheavals of the Russian Revolution he and some of his followers settled in Tbilisi in Georgia where in 1919 he founded the Institute for the Harmonious Development of Man. But the unsettled political situation forced him to move again to Istanbul where he and Ouspensky encountered the Mevlevi order of Sufis who practised 'turning' – these are the famous Whirling Dervishes.

In the early 1920s Gurdjieff was travelling and teaching in Western Europe where he finally re-established his Institute at Fontainebleau south of Paris. He had a near fatal car accident in 1924 but he slowly recovered (to the surprise of his doctors). He wrote several works, travelled to the US to teach and finally died on 29th October 1949. He is buried in the cemetery at Fontainebleau-Avon.

Gurdjieff taught that, although we move around and speak and earn a living, we are all, in fact, asleep and that our perception of the world is totally subjective and dreamlike. Ordinary life is unreal; truth and freedom lie in waking up. If we were awake then conflict, war and cruelty would be impossible. He devised exercises, activities and practices to encourage his followers to wake up.

Gurdjieff's teaching is referred to variously as 'The Fourth Way' (a term popularised by Ouspensky and his followers) or simply 'The Work'. His methods were designed to make higher states of consciousness available. These methods focused the attention, and minimised daydreaming. Sometimes his methods were designed to shock people out of their dream so he has a reputation for eccentricity and unconventional behaviour.

Books: *Beelzebub's Tales to His Grandson; Meetings With Remarkable Men; Life is Real Only Then, When I am* – (unfinished).

The law of action

My final word on the number seven is from Gurdjieff. He set out a law of action which divided any activity into seven steps. This sequence had two gaps where the activity could go off course, or cease altogether. One of these gaps is between the third and fourth step and the other right at the end before the final step. To bridge the first gap one needs vigilance, fortitude and inner discipline. But the final step often needs a greater measure of energy, often involving external intervention.

Take a simple example: the gutters need painting and the decision has been made (finally) to do so. It requires the acquisition and organisation of materials; the initial preparatory steps; the careful and attentive application of paint; and tidying up afterwards. Within each of these activities and over the whole process there are certain points where the energies need to be reinvigorated to push through a barrier of lethargy or boredom (or satisfaction with a completed stage). Around our houses, in our places of work, or in our relationships we may notice a number of uncompleted tasks, where we stopped either at the gap between Gurdjieff's third and fourth step; or when the task was nearly complete, just short of the final step.

The first three steps to knowledge, freedom and happiness set out in *Yoga Vasishtha* form an initial group where guidance, protection and knowledge are needed because of the vulnerability of the aspirant. It is possible (and initially, useful) to cycle around these opening three steps without bridging the gap and moving to the fourth level. Movement into the fourth stage represents a major shift, where the aspirant has developed the inner resources to help him or her through the next three stages. The move to the final step is quite a move – the last great stride to ultimate freedom.

Completing the Final Step

Often it is the final step in our ordinary endeavours which seems the hardest to complete – where each brush is cleaned, washed, dried and put away in its proper place; the lids on all the paint tins are sealed and the tins are stacked; the ladder is in its correct position; the drop sheets folded and put away; and all of this done at the right time – that is, as soon as the painting has been completed – not two, six or twelve months later.

It may seem odd that drying the last spoon, closing the last drawer, replying to the last email, or folding the last pair of socks is a spiritual discipline. But we might ask ourselves: Why *don't* we complete the task? How many uncompleted tasks are there at home and the workplace? What is the feeling we get when a job is brought to absolute fulfilment? **Try Practice 1, on page 14.**

PRACTICE 1 ➤ ➤ ➤ ➤ ➤ ➤ ➤ ➤ ➤

Consider the many partially completed tasks and jobs which fill your day – even if a task is 99% complete it is only partially completed. Pick one or two of these tasks, perhaps one from home and one from work – emptying the dishwasher, or folding the washing, or tidying your desk at the end of a day's work. For a week, stick at these simple jobs until they are 100% complete.

Be vigilant for any reluctance to finish. If a sort of heaviness and boredom arises, be aware of the feeling – and complete the task anyway. Don't cut corners – rather look for extra little things which would really finish the job.

Note the feelings which arise when the task is complete. Get a feel for the sense of peace and happiness from a simple job done to perfection. You can gradually extend your repertoire.

HINT: Keep it simple; pick relatively easy tasks (putting away your socks, rather than re-roofing the house); and don't pick too many, just one or two to start with. (One way in which the ego keeps you dancing to its tune is to present an impossible list of tasks which you naturally fail to complete.)

•   •   •   •   •   •   •

Getting Started (and some pitfalls)

Experiences of Freedom

We can start our journey to increased freedom by looking at our own experience. We have all experienced *some* freedom and happiness in our lives. Most of us treasure the memory of those times when we felt the cares and burdens of life magically slip from our shoulders. It might have been a childhood moment of ineffable joy, or that crazy year of travelling through Europe after high school, or the early years of marriage when you had no money, but it didn't matter because you had each other.

Or it may have been when you looked up at the stars, or gazed at a beautiful sunset, or witnessed the birth of your child, when you experienced, beyond the shadow of a doubt that there was something great hidden from ordinary view. And if you had then read one of the many descriptions of universal bliss by the master teachers of mankind you would have said, 'Yes, I recognise that and I could have written those words myself.'

About forty years ago, when I was about ten, I was sitting at a bus stop opposite a park in suburban Sydney on my way to school. As I was idly looking at the trees, one of them suddenly shone with an inner light. Seeing that light I felt universal, and limitless, and completely connected with a vast life force. After a few moments the feeling faded, but for years afterwards I would sneak a look at that same tree to see if that doorway would open for me again.

We often keep experiences like these to ourselves, squirrelling them away and pondering them in our hearts. And we remain quietly vigilant for another such moment, or for someone who can explain what happened and, perhaps, can help us find it again.

The Search Begins

When I was fourteen a teacher at my high school told me of a man giving a lecture at the Sydney Town Hall that Sunday. It was Krishnamurti and my chief memory is of being in the presence of someone who knew how things really worked, and who could explain those inner workings. I felt warmed and comforted by the knowledge that such a man existed. In retrospect I can say that a lifelong search began at that moment to find a teacher of my own.

This search for meaning and knowledge can go on at a level hidden from the seeker. As in my own case, when I eventually found a source of wisdom, many earlier steps in my life suddenly made sense: books I had read, people I had been drawn to, snippets of knowledge I had filed away. At sixteen, for example, out of the blue it came to mind that I should meditate – I had no background, training or technique so I just sat down for twenty minutes and repeated OM silently in my mind.

The fleeting moments of higher consciousness which many of us experience seem random and unpredictable. Can we find a way to make them permanent and accessible? Do these ways involve withdrawal from worldly responsibilities and rewards? Do we have to don robes and wander with a staff and begging bowl, with an expression of other-worldly detachment across the high Himalayas – perhaps with a mystic sound track playing in the background. Or is there a way which a normal man or woman can follow, while raising the kids, holding down a job, watching TV and generally getting on with life?

Ego - the barrier to freedom - and what he is telling you

The short answer is yes, there is such a way. The wise tell us repeatedly that permanent freedom and happiness are readily available to anyone who really wants it. Why then is this not our experience? It is simply because we prefer familiar habitual, 'comfortable' bondage and misery to unfamiliar, chancy freedom and happiness. Why? It is because our ego fights tenaciously, sneakily, underhandedly, beguilingly for its continued existence. Greed is its handmaiden, fear and anger its weapons of choice, illusion its territory – where it has 'hometown advantage'. And it has a knack for telling us disheartening and enthralling things in a series of voices, all of which sound just like us.

Imagine you have a companion who follows you around all day and talks non-stop, telling you how stupid you are, how foolish, dumb, jealous, irritated, right, wrong; commenting on other people, saying that they should be like this or that, or should act just as you require them; and then, for a change of pace, this 'friend' dredges up horrible memories from the past; or paralyses you with fear by recounting all the terrible things lurking in your future.

Well, if you did have such a friend you would be foolish to put up with him for a minute. Even if occasionally he said something nice just to keep you dangling, you would do all within your power to get rid of him, and you would count yourself lucky when he finally disappeared.

In fact, we all *do* have such a companion: he is our ego. But we *don't* move heaven and earth to banish him. Why? Simply because we believe our ego is us. And therefore we fight tooth and nail to defend him. When ego is under threat, *we* are under threat; if he goes, *we* go; if he dies, *we* die.

Ego has the beguiling power to make us believe that all these voices in our head are our own voice; and the things he tells us seem powerful and all-encompassing: I am a failure; I don't deserve to be happy or loved or taken seriously; I know nothing; I am worthless; I don't deserve to live. And ego also has a brassy pseudo-positive voice as well: Aren't I great; I deserve to be praised, gimme gimme gimme, look at me, look at me, look at me!

When we begin to seek inner stillness and peace we meet this unceasing, insistent mental cacophony. No wonder we cram our lives with superficial, fleeting pleasures and shy away from stillness and silence; filling our external world with constant music, radio, TV, even alcohol, drugs and other stimulation so there is no risk of a moment's genuine peace and quiet.

So what is this ego? It is an amalgam of deeply felt emotions reflective of both dark and light: infatuations, opinions, greed, fear, anger, arrogance; and these feelings are manufactured in a vicious circle which weaves our false sense of self, and which then enlists our aid to preserve its existence. An example: If you are a plumber and your plumbing skills are called into question, ego reacts; if your plumbing is praised, ego reacts. The reactions appear different but they are both ego. The problem is that your emotional state and sense of self seem to depend on how well the toilets flush. Hmmm.

It is ego which says, 'I am a plumber', and then bristles at criticism, and preens in the light of praise. Detachment from these limiting beliefs and feelings is a key step on the way to freedom and happiness. Be the best plumber in the world, but don't sell your birthright for efficient drains. What is this birthright which ego hides?

The True Self – Our Help and Guidance

Beyond ego is another Self. This Self is unchanging, observant and awake. It is the 'you' you have always been, while your body, mind and feelings have changed constantly from the moment you were born, walked, went to school, fell in love, got a job. Throughout all these changes you have always been yourself – never someone else.

Who is that 'you' who has never changed?

It is your true Self. It is the source of knowledge, insight, compassion and empathy. It is hidden by ego and his henchmen: fear, doubt, greed – and concern about being a plumber. If we could but take that journey through our own heart of darkness, past our ego, we would come through to an inner world of light and strength and peace. This inner journey through a hostile land to ultimate freedom is frequently referred to in the works of philosophy and scripture: walking through the valley of the shadow of death, or the valley of dry bones, or avoiding whited sepulchres. These allegories indicate a challenging journey through our own feelings including fear, small self-image, doubt and pain.

The encouraging news is that all the energy and fortitude we need to commence and succeed in attaining true and lasting happiness lies within our grasp. This is the energy we presently give to these spurious fears and doubts; and one of the initial tasks in going free is to unlock this conscious energy. This happens under the guidance available at the very first of the seven steps to freedom known as Good Impulse. In the ancient language Sanskrit, this is called *shubhech-cha*.

This help and guidance links us to our higher Self. While the voice of the false self is all too evident, the voice of the higher Self, while quieter, *never* goes away. It is the voice we hear when, occasionally, the ego shuts up, revealing memories and experiences of depth, stillness, peace and universal consciousness. It is this voice which is calling all of us. Many great teachings speak of these two contrasting voices – the shrill insistence of the ego and the quiet inner voice of the true self:

> *And, behold, the Lord passed by, and a great and strong wind rent the mountains, and brake in pieces the rocks before the Lord, but the Lord was not in the wind: and after the wind an earthquake; but the Lord was not in the earthquake: And after the earthquake a fire; but the Lord was not in the fire: and after the fire a still small voice.*[7]

Freedom From Limitations

To hear this inner voice and to be free of ego we need to address intelligently, systematically and effectively those aspects within ourselves which we would be better off without. Our aim is to be free of these limitations. This is true freedom. Freedom is not a positive condition. If you have a splitting headache and it goes away, what is this new state but simply the absence of a headache? We rarely walk around in a headache-free condition telling all our friends and congratulating ourselves on our unheadachey-ness.

We have all the tools we need to embark on this process of throwing out our unwanted mental and emotional baggage. The challenge is to pick these tools up and use them. Some of these mental and emotional tools are: attention, focus, reason, love and fortitude, and above all the consistent desire to be free. Some of the more unlikely tools are irritation, anger and fear. If we can turn our anger against those binding and limiting thoughts which cripple us, and tell those self-critical thoughts to get lost, then we will make a good start.

FACT BOX   Lester Levenson

Lester Levenson (1910–1994) was an American physicist, engineer and businessman, who, at the age of forty-two in 1952 had reached a point of catastrophic ill-health and misery despite having relationships and wealth. He had had a second coronary and had been, essentially, sent home to die.

Sitting in his apartment, depressed and frightened, he resolved to discover what

---

[7] I Kings 19:11–12.

he truly wanted from life. Thus began a three-month process where he discovered the core blockages to universal wisdom: desire for love and approval; desire for control and change; desire for eternal life and the fear of death; and ego. He released these desires and went completely free and then devised a method by which others could also go free which he called Releasing or the Sedona Method (he ended up in Sedona, Arizona hence the name).

Two of his chief students, Hale Dwoskin and Larry Crane, both offer courses and guidance in this method.

FACT BOX John Wren-Lewis

John Wren-Lewis (1923–2006) was an Australian scientist with conventionally sceptical views on mysticism and spiritual experiences until in 1983 he was poisoned in Thailand by a would-be thief and nearly died. When he came back to consciousness in a grimy hospital in Bangkok he discovered to his surprise that he was in an enlightened state, which he described years later as follows:

> I've been liberated from what William Blake called obsession with *futurity,* which, until it happened, I used to consider a psychological impossibility. And to my continual astonishment, for ten years now this liberation has made the conduct of practical life more rather than less efficient, precisely because time consciousness isn't overshadowed by *anxious thought for the morrow.*[8]

This is a further description by John Wren-Lewis of the enlightened state:

> . . . it is all still here, both the shining dark void and the experience of myself coming into being out of, yet somehow in response to, that radiant darkness. My whole consciousness of myself and everything else has changed. I feel as if the back of my head has been sawn off so that it is no longer the 60-year-old John who looks out at the world, but the shining dark infinite void that in some extraordinary way is also 'I.' And what I perceive with my eyes and other senses is a whole world that seems to be coming fresh-minted into existence *moment by moment,* each instant evoking the utter delight of 'Behold, it is very good.' Here yet again I am constantly up against paradox when I try to describe the experience. Thus, in one sense, I feel as if I am infinitely far back in sensing the world, yet at the same time I feel the very opposite, as if my consciousness is no longer inside my head at all, but out there in the things I am experiencing ... .[9]

[8] http://www.geocities.com/jiji_muge/dazzdark.html
[9] http://www.spiritualteachers.org/john_wren_lewis.htm

FACT BOX — Eckhart Tolle

Eckhart Tolle, born in Germany in 1948, grew up in Spain until he was nineteen then moved to London. He was subject to near suicidal depression and experienced what he described as 'inner transformation' at the age of twenty-nine where he fell into a deep darkness and emerged in a state of realisation or enlightenment. He spent some years assimilating this experience and since 1995 has lived in Vancouver.

His key teachings are contained in *The Power of Now* and *A New Earth,* which expound the way to transformation of consciousness and spiritual awakening through transcendence of our ego-based consciousness.

FACT BOX — Byron Katie

Byron Katie (born 1942) from Southern California, like Eckhart Tolle became depressed and was in a downward spiral of 'depression, rage, self-loathing, and constant thoughts of suicide; for the last two years she was often unable to leave her bedroom.' In 1986 she experienced a transformational moment which she describes as 'waking up to reality'.

Again in her words she described her discovery:

> I discovered that when I believed my thoughts, I suffered, but that when I didn't believe them, I didn't suffer, and that this is true for every human being. Freedom is as simple as that. I found that suffering is optional. I found a joy within me that has never disappeared, not for a single moment. That joy is in everyone, always.

She now teaches her method which she calls The Work.

Perseverance

COME BACK WHEN YOU'RE READY

A young man went to a holy man to seek liberation. The holy man asked him to go for a walk to the river. He then asked him to wade into the water. When they were waist deep the holy man plunged the fellow's head under the water and held him down. He finally let him up spluttering and gasping for breath. The holy man said to the would-be disciple, 'When you want freedom as much as you wanted that next breath, come back to me.'

We may not presently feel the need for freedom at quite that level, but we have to start somewhere. Even if that desire is not as passionate as the guru in the story required, the important thing is still to want freedom; and to stick at it, to persevere. Anything worthwhile – learning a foreign language, a new sport or any other skill – takes time and effort. If we can be patient and persistent with, say, French, and give the requisite time and energy to it, is it unreasonable to come at existential freedom and unending bliss similarly ready to put in the necessary time and attention?

To be sure there are instances of instantaneous enlightenment like St Paul on the road to Damascus. And more recently Lester Levenson, John Wren-Lewis, Eckhardt Tolle and Byron Katie, who have gone on to do magnificent work in guiding others to break free of pain and misery. It is a bit chancy however for us either to sit back and wait to be mugged by the Universe, or to do an exercise or two and then complain that the radiant light of supreme bliss isn't yet shining from every pore. So while a strong desire to be free is a prerequisite to gaining freedom, patience and persistence in applying practices and techniques are also necessary.

Mark Twain said: 'habit is habit and is not to be flung out of the window by any man, but coaxed downstairs a step at a time'. Basically we need to take the time to retrain ourselves. Those ego-based feelings which define our sense of self persist in the very cells of our body. They have a physiologically measurable effect. We might accept a need to make some adjustments to our lives, to jettison some troublesome habits and to ramp up the more virtuous aspects of our nature. But it is the deepest recesses and the ingrained habitual responses that we need to retrain. This does not often happen overnight. Habit is strong and patience, gentle persistence and resolve are our allies in achieving our final goals.

Self-limiting Beliefs

We all have self-limiting beliefs which control our lives from within and which tell us who we are, what we like and dislike, what we can and can't do, what we will put up with and what we won't tolerate and so on. These limiting beliefs also seem to attract the external circumstances which reinforce that same belief system. A simple and obvious example: if we hate a certain behaviour we will be sensitive and alert to it; and we may complain bitterly that the world is full of fools and knaves. Others, who are less inclined to worry or even notice, will be serenely unaware of the mortal dangers they avoided.

Most of us have friends who time and again create their own catastrophic circumstances, reinforcing their prejudices, setting the cycle in a deepening groove of habitual behaviour. They may be repeatedly cheated in business; they may be on to their third marriage to a spouse who is a precise match of the previous two; they may move on to their umpteenth job because, yet again, the boss is a dangerous lunatic. Is it fate, or accident, or might it be caused in part by their own self-limiting beliefs? These beliefs do have the power to create our circumstances and they don't disappear simply because we want them to. Hence the need to persevere and to be patient on the way to freedom.

Changing Our Habits

Our habits, and our self-image rule our lives. If we really want to change, grow and break free it is at this level of deep thought and feeling that we have to begin. The initial work we do at the first three steps on the way to freedom is largely concerned with reducing the pull of habitual beliefs and behaviour. Persistence, patience, fortitude, grit and a bit of intelligent focus is essential; as well as an inner emotional vocabulary to deal with both success and failure: a good start is to go lightly on the self-congratulations when your efforts are successful; and to avoid self-criticism when you slip up. Both success and failure are inevitable and both are equally false friends.

Focus on the Essential Goal

Focus on the essentials is also helpful. A friend of mine was helping out at a study and meditation retreat. He was preparing for a tea break and had to go to the other end of the building to get some more milk. As he turned a corner he saw the corridor was filled with a glorious, ineffable golden light, radiating consciousness and bliss. He knew he could enter that golden blissful light by reaching out and touching it. But he knew it would distract him, that he would get lost in it, so he kept walking down the corridor because his job was to get milk for those students who wanted a cup of tea.

In the pursuit of spiritual riches one should never forget one's basic humanity, and remain intent on a higher duty to feed the hungry, serve water to the thirsty and cheer up the downhearted.

There is another reason for resisting these glittering temptations. Golden chains are just as binding as iron chains. We can just as easily get lost in a dream as in a nightmare. (In fact more easily – the nightmare has inbuilt motivation to wake us up.) In Chapter Three I will discuss more fully this need to surrender the pleasant experiences.

STOPPING THE FAST

On the holiest day of the Jewish year, the Day of Atonement, when the congregation fasts all day, a great Rabbi was leading the closing prayer when he received a spiritual insight – if he kept the prayers going just a few minutes longer two things would happen: the Messiah would come and redeem mankind; but he also knew that one old man, weakened by fasting, would die. He immediately brought the prayers to an end.

While we are unlikely to be confronted with so dramatic a choice, the meaning for us is clear, don't sacrifice common sense or your basic humanity for some perception of spiritual gain. But the way is signposted with little rewards. These seem to come out of the blue and are designed to encourage us to keep going.

GOD IS LIKE A FATHER

Another Jewish story tells of a student who went to a Rabbi and asked why sometimes he felt God was so close he could almost touch Him and, at other times He felt very distant.

The Rabbi said God was like a loving father teaching His son to walk. He holds out His hands on either side of the toddler so he won't fall and calls him to walk towards Him. As the toddler approaches the father withdraws to build up his strength. Every now and then He lets the baby reach Him and gives him a warm hug to reward him and encourage his efforts.

In the face of these occasional insights and rewards we need to be reasonable. Another man I knew described seeing a window he was cleaning turn into radiant jewels of light. And he spoke of this with despondency because he knew, so he said, that he would have to wait months or years to experience it again; and soon after he gave up on his work on self-awareness.

Honesty and Humility

Other qualities we need, therefore, are honesty with ourselves, and a little humility in the face of our limitations. In this pursuit of freedom we certainly need guidance, help and knowledge from those who have walked the path before us; but ultimately the only person we have to answer to is the one who looks back at us from the bathroom mirror. And it is sometimes surprisingly difficult to admit weakness or failure to that person. In *The Wisdom of the Enneagram* Hudson and Riso alert us to our egoic tendency to think our actions spring from a higher, healthier level than the one from which they actually come.[10] Kohlberg, who developed a taxonomy of moral development, pointed out that we can all talk the talk a level or two above where we walk the walk.

We may like to think that we would be scrupulously honest when faced with temptation; that we would not favour a friend when called upon to judge an issue; that we would speak the truth when we felt we might be ridiculed, or worse. We might even criticise those who have failed to live up to these lofty standards. But can we say for sure that, when we have been weighed in the balance, we won't be found wanting? A little humility is a marvellous corrective to the pressures of the ego. **See Practice 2, page 26.**

Knowledge

I will assume that you, the reader, want to be free and happy; and you want this freedom and happiness to be long lasting; that you believe such long-lasting freedom and happiness is possible of attainment; that you are

---

[10] DR Riso & R Hudson, *The Wisdom of the Enneagram,* Bantam Books, New York, 1999, p. 78.

willing to put in some work; and that you understand that work involves persistent, patient and honest effort.

So how do we find the required information and knowledge to help us along the way? Sometimes it is not the unavailability of knowledge, but its overabundance which flummoxes us. Where do we start? How do we gain entry into so wide a world with so much to offer. Do we have to spend decades studying Sanskrit, or Persian, or Biblical Hebrew to penetrate the true depths of the Vedas, or the Sufi mystics, or the Kabbalah? Is every path right for us? Does every doorway lead to our goal? Will we find an authentic master or fall in with a charlatan?

My advice here is to keep looking until you find a system or path which suits your nature and feels right. In the meantime I offer in this book a system which I have found consistently useful and which has led me to higher and higher levels of conscious awareness.

I have found the particular system set out in this book both practical and useful because it covers the whole journey, from the initial stirrings of the desire to be free to the state of union with the universe. The seven steps to freedom don't exclude other disciplines and practices; study of this system includes aspects of many others and can be illuminating to anyone seeking the ultimate goal.

PRACTICE 2 ➤ ➤ ➤ ➤ ➤ ➤ ➤ ➤ ➤

Useless and idle and destructive speech are some of the ego's favourite weapons. It uses them to cement its control over us.

Some forms of negative speech are: destructive criticism; speaking when no one is listening; idle repetition; speaking as if you know something when you don't; speaking to overwhelm or intimidate or to silence others with your opinions; hasty words which are needlessly hurtful; lying. This is not an exhaustive list, but should alert you to listen for speech which is basically harmful to yourself and others.

Resolve to curb some of the more extreme forms of idle speech. This is not meant to interfere with light, social chat and friendly interactions. We can recognise harmful speech by the sour taste it leaves in our mouths and how it makes us feel.

The key is to listen and 'be there' when you're speaking (not as easy as it sounds). If you hear yourself indulging in this type of speech the simple remedy is to stop. (If necessary tell the people you're talking to why you have stopped speaking.)

Chapter **One**

Step One:
Good Impulse

CASE STUDY **ONE**

A young woman has just graduated from university and is about to embark on a prosperous and successful career. She is sporty, interested in literature and theatre and has a close family and circle of friends. But her teenage years were not easy. Throughout that gawky, awkward time everyone else seemed more confident, able and attractive. And despite her present popularity, academic success and professional achievements, a sense of inadequacy haunts her. All her accomplishments never seem enough. As she compares her life, her looks, her intelligence to others, in her own mind, she comes off second best.

One day leafing through a volume of Shakespeare's Sonnets she comes across a few lines:

Yet in these thoughts myself almost despising,
Haply I think on thee, – and then my state,
Like to the lark at break of day arising
From sullen earth, sings hymns at heaven's gate.[11]

She wonders about 'haply I think on thee'. Is it God, a lover, a teacher? A desire arises in her heart to find such a 'thee' and she

---

[11] William Shakespeare, Sonnet 29.

signs up for a course of self-enquiry which she has been meaning
to join for years.

CASE STUDY **TWO**

A young man without much formal education is hitchhiking with
his girlfriend around the country, surfing and sleeping on the beach.
He works in cafés and bars, washing dishes to fund this 'career'. It
is an apparently idyllic life for a young man. But satisfaction eludes
him. He has a niggling feeling that there has to be more to life. One
day he is cleaning the kitchen floor when his eye is caught by a
scrap of newspaper advertising a course in self-awareness. A light
switches on inside him. He and his girlfriend enrol in the course.

CASE STUDY **THREE**

Tragedy strikes a young couple when their baby dies of cot death.
Consumed by grief they question the meaning and purpose of life.
The mother calls a friend of her sister whom she has hardly ever
spoken to beyond mere pleasantries. But there was something
about her which was somehow different and the mother knows she
is into some form of yoga or meditation. Wanting to talk to someone steady, on impulse she gets in touch with her.

Shubhech-cha

What do these stories have in common? First, our young graduate, the
surfer, the grieving mother, all have a sense that there is something missing
in their lives. Secondly they desire to find out more; and thirdly they come
across someone who may be able to provide an answer.

These three stories illustrate the first step on the way to freedom.
The Sanskrit name for this step is *shubhech-cha* (pronounced *shoob hech
ch'ha*). *Shubha* means good or pure; and *ich-cha* means wish, desire or
inclination. The English word *ask* is derived from the root form of *ich-cha*.

According to Vasishtha, this compound word means a pure wish or intention, and is translated as Good Impulse.

We Need to Ask

To be receptive to this good impulse we have to feel an inner need to move beyond our present condition. If we don't have a question, a sense of dissatisfaction or loss, all the wisdom of the ages won't help us. You may have met a wise man or woman – you may even have spoken to him or her. But the wise don't generally proclaim themselves, or initiate action or intervene in our lives unless there is a need or an openness or a question. Jesus warned his followers not to throw pearls before swine – a rather graphic and unflattering image of those whose ears are not yet ready to hear.

Rather than trying to wake us up, the wise wait for us to stir in our sleep and ask for help. This asking, however, doesn't need to be particularly skilful or erudite. There are many stories where a wise person is wandering along and finds someone lost in misery and tears, and they offer a helping hand – it is the tears which are the call for help. Many of us don't have the appropriate vocabulary to ask for assistance. The wise don't initiate action, but they are vigilant to help those in need, and those who are ready to follow their advice.

Arjuna's plight on the battlefield (see page 8) is the same as ours: we are caught between the forces of good and evil and are unsure what to do and we don't appear to have access to our life's charioteer, nor do we have the words to ask for help. But asking is a necessary precondition to the first step on the way to ultimate freedom. And humility is a great help. **See Practice 3, page 49.**

Standing at the Crossroads

The people in the case studies were standing at a crossroads in their lives. They could keep going in the direction that life had laid out for them: family, career, money, success; or failure, loneliness, isolation and poverty; or some mix of the two. This sort of life is essentially governed by the past, where we try, often unconsciously, to make each day as similar to yesterday as possible. Shakespeare describes the emptiness and ultimate futility of such a life:

Tomorrow, and tomorrow, and tomorrow.
Creeps in this petty pace from day to day
To the last syllable of recorded time;
And all our yesterdays have lighted fools
The way to dusty death. Out, out, brief candle!
Life's but a walking shadow, a poor player,
That struts and frets his hour upon the stage,
And then is heard no more; it is a tale
Told by an idiot, full of sound and fury,
Signifying nothing.[12]

Such a life is reactive: something happens – a pay rise, a harsh word, a chance meeting; and there is a matching response – momentary happiness, an even harsher criticism, a new friendship. And life goes on: a successful career, a divorce, a widening circle of acquaintance. And we wait for the next external event to delight or dismay us.

The Road Less Travelled

At a crossroads we can choose a different path in life which leads to freedom. The Katha Upanishad speaks of 'diverging roads: one called ignorance, the other wisdom'[13]; one leading to death and the other to eternal life. John Bunyan wrote the whole of *Pilgrim's Progress* to illustrate the many opportunities, traps and pitfalls on the path to salvation. The Bible tells us:

Enter ye in at the strait gate: for wide is the gate, and broad is the way, that leadeth to destruction, and many there be which go in thereat: because straight is the gate, and narrow is the way, which leadeth unto life, and few there be that find it. [14]

---

[12] William Shakespeare, *Macbeth,* act 5, scene 5.

[13] Sri Purohit Swami & WB Yeats, *The Ten Principal Upanishads,* Faber & Faber Ltd, London, 1975, p. 29.

[14] Matthew 7:13–14.

Although this path to freedom is for the few, there is no reason why you should not be one of them. Someone has to be. The decision is there for any individual to grasp the opportunity to go free, to respond to the good impulse and take the first of the seven steps on the way to freedom and happiness.

And how do we take the first step on this road less travelled? First we need the desire: to be free, to know more, to be more alive, to have control and autonomy. Secondly we need to meet someone who can give us direction. And, thirdly we need to be willing to follow their guidance.

Don't Look Back!

But first: a cautionary note. Traditional stories and legends tell of heroes or heroines pursuing their quest along dark and dangerous paths where they meet, sometimes in surprising or unattractive guise, a helper who warns them to stick to the path, avoid the food, not to talk to strangers, not to fall asleep, not to unlock the door, and not to look back.

And what do they do? Despite all our cries of frustration, they leave the path, eat the food, and talk to the first stranger to appear, they lie down just to close their eyes for a few minutes, they unlock the door to take a quick peek or look back just to make sure. Orpheus looked back and lost Eurydice; Lot's wife looked back and was turned into a pillar of salt; Odysseus's crew slew the sheep of the Sun God when they were specifically told not to; they opened the sack of the wind god Aeoleus thinking it was treasure and were blown away from their home when it was in sight; the pilgrim Christian took shortcuts or failed to heed the advice of those sent to help him, and ended up in the Slough of Despond and Doubting Castle in the clutches of the Giant Despair.

And all these stories are *our* stories.

THE CITY OF SEVEN GATES

There is a tale of a king who lived in a city of seven walls with seven gates. One day he sent out a proclamation saying that he would give his kingdom to the one who came to his throne room at a certain time on a certain day to claim it. He said, further, that the gates would be open and the guards instructed to allow anyone through. To some suspicious souls this seemed too good to be true. Others were not interested in becoming king. Some didn't hear or understand the announcement, while others just ignored it. And some were too infirm or too distant or too lazy to make the journey.

But, as the day approached, thousands did come to claim the kingdom. As they approached the city they saw, at the first gate, refreshments laid out for all those who had made the journey and were thirsty. Many thought that they would lose nothing by stopping to have something to drink. Others however were eager to get to the throne room at the appointed hour so they pressed on.

At the second gate, food in abundance was set out on tables, freely available to all who were hungry. While many continued on, some stopped to have a quick snack. At the third gate there were amusements, games and entertainments. Some thought that no harm could come of watching the jugglers and the dancing girls. At the fourth gate there were basins with water and soap and towels for the dusty travellers to wash and clean themselves. Some thought, after all, it would be unfitting to take over the kingdom all travel-stained and dusty from the journey, so they stopped at this gate to wash.

At the fifth gate there was money by the sack load. Some thought of the expense of their journey and thought it only fair that they should be reimbursed. A few made it to the sixth gate where jewels were spilling out of chests. Their eyes lit up as they began to fill their pockets with sapphires, rubies, emeralds and diamonds.

Very few made it to the seventh gate where shaded canopies covered comfortable beds with fresh linen sheets and down-filled pillows, and they could not resist the lure of a short rest – after all there was still plenty of time before the appointed hour.

Just before the time expired however a determined young man appeared at the first gate and without a sideways glance he walked past the drink, the food, the entertainment, the bathing facilities, the money and the jewels and shut his ears to the sounds of snoring coming from the canopied beds. He walked into the king's throne room and asked for the kingdom which was freely given to him. He took his place on the throne and then ordered his guards to arrest and imprison all those who were drinking his wine and eating his food, watching his entertainment without paying, taking his money and jewels and sleeping in his beds.

The Need for Action

Couldn't all the others resist temptation? Why couldn't Orpheus, Christian and the others stick to the instructions? If they wanted the kingdom why were they beguiled by food and drink? If it were us, we wouldn't be so foolish. Hmm, possibly.

If we feel keen to set out on the way to freedom, we will soon have the opportunity to find out if we will succumb to temptation and distraction rather than keep walking the path. At this stage of Good Impulse we have to act, we have to do something, we have to embark on our journey and this brings tests and temptations.

THE PRODIGAL SON

The story of the prodigal son in St Luke's Gospel[15] *illustrates all aspects of the seven steps to freedom including the need for some action at this first stage.*

This parable tells of a wealthy father who had two sons. One day the younger of the two asked for his inheritance and the father divided his living between the two of them. Not long afterwards the younger son set out to a far country and there 'wasted his substance on riotous living'. A famine arose in the land and the son, having nothing left, was hungry and no one was willing to give him anything. So he joined himself to a citizen of that land and took a job feeding swine. But he was so hungry he was tempted to eat 'the husks that the swine did eat'.

Then as Luke tells us 'he came to himself', remembered his father's house, and how the servants had plenty to eat. He resolved to return to his father's house and throw himself on his father's mercy. After this awakening the prodigal son actually took his first step towards home. And the story tells us 'he arose'. This is his first small step to redemption, and illustrates the need to take some action.

The story goes on to tell us that when he was still a great way off his father ran to meet him, clothed him in a fine robe, put a ring on his finger and ordered up a feast to celebrate the return of his son who was lost but was now found, who was dead but was now alive again.

---

[15] Luke 15:11–32.

As a postscript, the older brother who dutifully stayed behind heard the celebration and when he was told of the party he became angry. After all he had worked all this time but he never had a party. The father again went out and assured his elder son that all that he had was his and that it was proper that they celebrate the return of the prodigal.

FACT BOX — Plato

Plato (424 BC – 348 BC) was an Athenian philosopher and disciple of Socrates. He was also Aristotle's teacher. These three men essentially laid the foundations of Western philosophical thought and therefore were key figures in giving the West its distinct world outlook which values individual responsibility and liberty, rational enquiry and creative disputation.

Born into an aristocratic Athenian family he became a follower of Socrates and laid out his teaching in thirty-five dialogues and thirteen letters (the authenticity of some is disputed). He founded the first Western institution of higher learning known as the Academy.

Plato expounded the idea that beyond the perceptible world of the senses and action, there is another world which is more real and substantial. For example, behind all beautiful objects – flowers, sunsets, music – there is Beauty itself which is complete, untainted and perfect and from which all individual beautiful objects draw some of their partial beauty. Similarly with all universal principles which he called 'Ideas' – such as Courage, Justice, Wisdom, and so on. These Ideas exist in substantial perfection and all perceptible examples of them (a courageous action, a just decision, a wise thought) merely partake of them in some measure.

He believed that man was fundamentally immortal, limitless and free, while seeming mortal, limited and bound. And that a man could attain freedom through rational enquiry into truth – a process called dialectic. The highest form of dialectic becomes a sort of meditation on and a merging with the universal Ideas.

Of course, in the dialogues and letters he addresses himself to a vast range of issues and ideas and worked his way through various conclusions. A good starting point is to obtain a good translation of Plato's dialogue called *The Republic* and reserve some time to curl up with it.

PLATO'S CAVE

Imagine prisoners in an underground cave chained by the neck and ankles from birth.[16] Unable to turn their heads they can only watch the back wall of the cave. Behind and above them is a great blazing fire which throws the prisoners' shadows on the back wall. Between the prisoners and the fire is a raised walkway with a screen along which are walking men carrying cut out shapes of various objects – trees, animals, clouds, houses and so on. Some of these men talk and some are silent. Some of the prisoners talk and discuss the order of the shadows. The voices echo off the back wall and, knowing no other reality, the prisoners take the shadows to be real and think the echoed voices they hear are coming from the shadows.

Now imagine that a liberator appears and he strikes the chains from one of the prisoners, forces him to stand and turn and look at the blazing fire. His eyes are in pain and he cannot see because of the brightness of the light. Gradually the prisoner's eyes adjust and he can see the objects being carried on the walkway. He sees that they are much more real than the shadows which he previously took to be the only reality.

Then the liberator takes the freed prisoner past the fire to a steep and narrow tunnel leading out of the cave. Again the prisoner is blinded, now by being plunged into darkness. The way is steep and rocky and it is hard to climb so the liberator has to encourage and cajole him to keep going. When the prisoner emerges blinking into the light he is again dazzled and again it takes time for his eyes to adjust. At first he can only see the shadows of trees, animals, clouds and houses, then he can see them reflected in water and polished surfaces and then by moonlight. Finally he sees them in daylight and at last he can see the sun itself.

If then he would cast his mind back on his life in the dark shadow-world of the cave, and the honours that the prisoners heap on each other for knowing the order and shape of the shadows, he would hardly envy his former friends. If he were then to descend again into the cave to free others he would find himself blinded again by the half light in the cave and he would find the things which the prisoners valued to be valueless. His speech would mystify the prisoners and unsettle them. They would say to each other: 'Look what happened to him. Up he went and down he came, blinded and ignorant.'

---

[16] Plato, *The Republic*, Book VII.

And, Plato asks, if they could but lay hands on him would they not put him to death?

Glaucon, to whom Socrates is telling this story, says: 'You have shown me a strange image. And these are strange prisoners.' To which Socrates replies: 'Like ourselves.'

Plato's story of the cave is full of imagery and instruction for us, and it would take another whole book to tease out everything it had to say. For present purposes let's just take one obvious message from the story: the need for some form of action to begin our journey to freedom. The first action of the freed prisoner, helped by his liberator, is simply to stand up and turn and face the fire. In the following steps he needs his liberator to continue to help because the light blinds him and his eyes are in pain and then he is blinded by the darkness of the tunnel and so on. No wonder he is reluctant to continue, and needs guidance and help.

It would be remiss of me, however, not to temper this note of caution by telling of the many delights on the way to freedom, the help that comes from surprising quarters, and the sheer relief of knowing that life is getting better and better.

FACT BOX Leon MacLaren and the School of Economic Science

Leon MacLaren (1910–1994) was a barrister born in Glasgow, Scotland. In 1926 at the age of sixteen, he had an inspiration that truth and justice could be discovered, and, having been discovered, they could be taught to others. He resolved to start a school to do just that.

His father Andrew MacLaren was for nearly two decades the Labour Member of Parliament for Stoke-on-Trent in the British Midlands. MacLaren's initial vision, shaped by his father's zeal for economic justice during the Great Depression of the 1930s, was to study the true and just economic relations of people in society which, if implemented, would lead to prosperity and freedom – avoiding the Scylla of leftist state control, fascism and tyranny; and the Charybdis of ruthless free-wheeling capitalism.

In the 1930s he founded the School of Economic Science and, through the study of the work of American economist Henry George, MacLaren developed many useful and interesting insights into the proper arrangements for taxation, land ownership, economic rent and so on. But he soon found that economic relations were dependant on law and politics and that these, in turn, were governed by the laws governing human relations. By the 1950s, after some examination of these areas, it became clear to him that economics, law and politics were essentially dependent on human nature, and that he needed to start delving into the inner workings of the human spirit. In 1955 he began to present a course in Philosophy, in its original meaning of 'love of wisdom'. He came across the work of Ouspensky and the Study Society and found startling parallels between his work on economic justice, and their work on the inner spirit. Both organisations, along with many others, were seeking a living, enlightened teacher. They felt such a teacher had to exist but remained tantalisingly elusive. The arrival of the Maharishi Mahesh Yogi (see Fact Box page 41) in 1961 in London opened a pathway to such a master teacher.

The story, as told to me, was that Dr Francis Roles, Ouspensky's successor, rang Leon MacLaren one day in 1961 and said: 'MacLaren, an enlightened master has arrived in London. Go and check him out.' The Maharishi initiated the students of the School of Economic Science and the Study Society into a system of mantra meditation which immeasurably deepened their experience of inner stillness and knowledge. He also introduced them to his teacher, His Holiness Shri Shantananda Saraswati, the Shankaracharya of Jyoti Math who expounded the philosophy of Advaita Vedanta – the philosophy of non-dualism which proposes that the universe is constituted of nothing but consciousness and that all the individual forms and differences are illusory shapes, mere appearances on the face of consciousness. Like the figures in a dream, they appear real but when the dreamer awakes they disappear.

Over the next thirty years or so Leon MacLaren went to India many times to meet and converse with Shantananda Saraswati and the fruits of these conversations became the underpinning to the teaching of the School of Economic Science which offered courses to those interested in going free. Around the world branches of the SES – usually called Schools of Philosophy – were set up, including one in Sydney in 1967.

The School of Philosophy

When I was nineteen my brother told me of the School of Philosophy in Sydney, a school teaching self-awareness. He was keen that I should go along. I asked him what they talked about and he spoke about stillness and awareness and self-knowledge. I was, to be frank, only marginally interested. So I asked him the question I really wanted the answer to. Did they tell you why people lied? I could understand why someone would, say, tell a teacher they had done their homework, when they hadn't, if they thought they could get away with it. There was an obvious advantage in this sort of lie.

But the lies I was eager to find out about, and which used to infuriate me when I told them, were those which had no pay off. I would say I knew something which I knew nothing about, or boast of having done something I had never done, or exaggerate needlessly. Some time later I heard a man describe the exact situation. He had been in the city when a tourist had asked for directions. He said: 'I gave them directions even though I had no idea where they should go. Just to be helpful!' This was the sort of thing I wanted to be free of.

In 1975 I signed up for the introductory philosophy course in Sydney and to my delight the School gave practical help in overcoming this tendency. My desire to be free had met a helping hand – I now knew of a place where I could find answers. The course outlined several forms of useless speech, all of which keep us under the thumb of the ego: speaking as if we know something when we don't; useless repetition; destructive criticism – both of ourselves and others – and speaking when no one is listening. **See Practice 2, page 26.**

Finding Guidance

If you have that frustrating feeling that there must be something more to life, how do you find guidance? How can you find someone who knows what's going on and can explain it to you? The answer is unique to each individual. The comforting words of a local priest will help one person, while the all-encompassing love of an eastern guru will do it for another. Shakespeare or Mozart may set one person on the quest, while the intriguing stillness and confidence of an acquaintance will start another asking real questions. **See Practices 4 and 5, page 50.**

FACT BOX   Guidance

The guidance of a teacher is, of course, the first step on our way. Western civilisation has produced an astonishing array of extraordinary men and women who have discovered the path to freedom and happiness. And they have left pointers for those who wish to follow in their footsteps. Their works – the Bible, Plato's Dialogues, Shakespeare's poetry and plays, and a host of other works – are still available. But we, in the West, seem to be at a phase of our history where the inner meaning of these works has become harder to access. As an indicator of how beneficent the universe is, in these days when many of us have difficulty hearing wisdom in our own language and tradition, we in the West have historically unprecedented access to the works and teachings of a rich variety of sages, gurus and masters from other civilisations.

How did this come about? At the end of the nineteenth century the material wealth, power and success of the Victorian era prompted many people, paradoxically, to begin looking for greater inner meaning. Many travelled the world to find a living source of wisdom. The trauma and massive loss of life in the First World War, and the anguish of parents and wives and siblings who had lost loved ones also triggered interest in the 'spirit world'. Well-known figures such as Sir Arthur Conan Doyle, author of the Sherlock Holmes books, became interested in these areas. Other writers such as Pamela Travers, the author of the Mary Poppins books (read them again with this knowledge and they take on another dimension of meaning) and Katherine Mansfield, the novelist from New Zealand, studied under Gurdjieff. Frank Lloyd Wright also studied Gurdjieff's teachings. One of Gurdjieff's chief followers, Peter Ouspensky, founded his Society for the Study of Normal Human Psychology (now called the Study Society) in London to discover a system whereby men and women could come out of the sleep in which they were enmeshed. Gurdjieff and Ouspensky believed that, although we appear to be awake and to pursue productive lives, we are in fact asleep. Shakespeare in *The Tempest* describes this condition of 'waking sleep':

Sebastian:	What! Art thou waking?
Antonio:	Do you not hear me speak?
Sebastian:	I do: and surely it is a sleepy language, and thou speakest out of thy sleep. What didst thou say? This is a strange repose, to be asleep with eyes wide open; standing, speaking, moving and yet so fast asleep.

Gurdjieff and Ouspensky devised exercises and movements and practices to wake their students up. Sometimes these appeared to be pretty ruthless and a bit eccentric but the aim was wakefulness. After Ouspensky's death Dr Francis Roles took over the leadership of the Study Society.

At the same time Rudolph Steiner was developing the ideas of Anthroposophy, and Annie Besant, Charles Leadbetter and Madam Blavatsky were developing Theosophy. Krishnamurti, groomed to be the new messiah by the Theosophists, declined the offer and began teaching in his own way.

An interesting account of many of these early forays into the world of the spirit is contained in *God Is My Adventure* by Rom Landau.[17] Written in the 1930s it is an account of Landau's own search for meaning in the course of which he sought out all the teachers, gurus and messiahs of that rather unsettled time. Rather chillingly one of these 'messiahs' was Adolph Hitler – Landau was unimpressed:

The thin mouth under the little black moustache was shut tight and the face bore a strained and self-conscious expression. [18]

Leon MacLaren (see Fact Box, page 36) founded the School of Economic Science in 1937, studied with Dr Roles and both were introduced to meditation by Maharishi Mahesh Yogi (see Fact Box, page 41). The Maharishi's teacher Brahmananda, known as Guru Deva (The Beatles sing of him in the chorus of the song 'Across the Universe'), had been appointed Shankaracharya of the northern Indian seat of wisdom known as Jyotir Math. Brahmananda's successor, Shantananda Saraswati, was alive and well and in situ. Finally a living source of eternal wisdom had been found.

Dr Roles in 1961 and Leon MacLaren in 1965 went to India to meet Shantananda Saraswati and, in effect, became his disciples. The Study Society and the School of Economic Science maintained their relationship with this fount of wisdom for decades and benefited mightily from his direct guidance.

In the past few decades a myriad of similar teachings and systems have become available: yoga, meditation, chakra healing, emotional cleansing and so on. Some are firmly grounded in Buddhist, Vedic, Christian, Islamic or Jewish tradition. Others are more loosely connected to an orthodox tradition, but most draw their inspiration from the great ocean of wisdom as expressed by saints and sages throughout time. One thing is for sure: a great amount of guidance is available to anyone setting out on the path to freedom.

[17] R Landau, *God Is My Adventure,* Unwin, London, 1935.
[18] ibid. p. 160.

FACT BOX — Maharishi Mahesh Yogi

The Maharishi (1917–2008), Indian teacher and mystic, was most famous for introducing transcendental meditation to the West. He was a disciple of Swami Brahmananda Saraswati who was the Shankaracharya of Jyotir Math in Northern India from 1941 to 1953. Maharishi always credited Brahmananda (Guru Deva) as the inspiration of his teachings. Beginning his worldwide teaching in the late 1950s he became known particularly for inspiring Western celebrities, most notably The Beatles, and introducing them to meditation and other aspects of Indian spirituality.

For decades he taught transcendental meditation and set up centres around the world to train others to teach the system and to make it widely available. He also propounded systems of healing known as ayurveda and astrology known as jyotish. On his death Sir Paul McCartney and Ringo Starr along with many others issued statements of love and support.

FACT BOX — Adi Shankara and the Shankaracharyas

The title **'Shankaracharya'** is given to the occupant of each of four seats of wisdom founded in the North, South, East and West of India by **Adi Shankara** – or the original Shankara (788–820 AD). According to semi-legendary accounts he was born into a poor Brahmin family who were given the choice by the gods either of having a son who would live a long, but ordinary life; or a son who would be a *jagadguru* – a world teacher – but would only live for sixteen years. They chose the latter.

He was born at a time when orthodox forms of Hinduism had become atrophied and ritualistic and Buddhism was gaining popularity in India. Shankara propounded the philosophy of Advaita Vedanta – the philosophy of non-dualism which holds that everything is woven of a single pure consciousness and that all apparent differences of form are illusory. He taught that this philosophy of non-dualism was the basis of true religion.

He sought to reinvigorate traditional religion by travelling the length and breadth of India engaging the heads of rival schools of theology in formal debates. He defeated them all and each became his disciple. He also wrote copious commentaries on Indian sacred texts, including the Upanishads and the Bhagavad Gita, to uncover their hidden meaning and make them available to everyone. These commentaries are readily available in translation. In addition to this he wrote hymns for those of a devotional nature. Partly as a result of his work the various branches of Hinduism experienced a resurgence and Buddhism became marginalised in India.

To ensure the continued success of his work he founded the four seats of learning in India at the four points of the compass and appointed four of his chief disciples, known as Shakaracharyas, as the first occupants of these seats.

Legend has it that he died at the age of thirty-two because his work so pleased the gods that they granted him a further sixteen years of life.

Recognising the Teacher

If our desire to be free leads us to begin seeking a way forward how do we know when we have found an authentic guide? We might assume that we would know a holy man if one turned up. But scriptures and myths are full of stories where people miss the moment and fail to recognise the person they were fated to learn from. In these stories the seeker has to go through trials to retrieve the situation. The story of Parsifal and the Wounded Fisherman is a poignant example where he fails to free the Fisherman and attain the Holy Grail by asking about his wound.[19]

The people of Nazareth didn't recognise Jesus because they were too familiar with his father and mother, and brothers and sisters. They couldn't conceive that someone they had seen grow up and had lived with was the Son of God.[20] I once asked a class of children how they would react if one of their number disappeared for several years and then returned proclaiming himself to be the Messiah. Like the Nazarenes they expressed an understandable degree of scepticism.

Of course there are alternative accounts of seekers recognising their teacher even if somewhat disguised.

SHRI NAMADEVA AND THE DOG

Shri Namadeva was cooking bread over a fire and left the loaves outside to cool. When a dog ran off with one of the loaves in its mouth Namadeva set off in pursuit with a knife and butter calling, 'My Lord, my Lord! Don't

---

19 L Clarke, *Parzival and the Stone from Heaven,* HarperCollins, London, 2001, p. 84.
20 Matthew 13:53–58.

*you want butter with your bread?' The dog stopped and revealed himself
to be none other than the Lord Shri Krishna.*

*As Namadeva bowed to him, the Lord said, 'Namadeva, you recognised
me!'*

'How could I fail to?' asked Namadeva.

A friend of mine, after many years of meditation, study and discipline in
the School of Philosophy, went to a lecture given by Swami Tejomayananda,
the leader of the Chinmaya Mission. 'I took one look at him,' she said,
'and I fell in love. I knew I had met my teacher.' She now works with the
Mission in Melbourne.

But are all of us so confident in our ability to know a wise man when
we met him? Even if we did know what would we do then? A wonderful
lady of my acquaintance who had the privilege of sitting with Shantananda
Saraswati, the Shankaracharya of Jyotir Math in Northern India, told me
how at their first meeting she sat there making strenuous efforts to
experience fully the wonderful presence of this great man. She told me
how he had looked at her and, as she described it, 'It felt like he reached
out, picked me up and put me back into my body. He just wants you to
be yourself. Another thing,' she said, 'Don't think you can't dream off in
the presence of a holy man. I can tell you it's possible because I've done it!'
(I have too.)

The key advice is to be ready, open and vigilant – and patient. Perhaps
when you find your teacher, it will be as clear to you as it was to my friend
from Melbourne. If not, avoid cherry picking at too many different options;
and after a reasonable period of investigation, just follow the path your
own nature lays out. The wise know what we need, and they are ready
to help anyone who will respond to the seeds of wisdom sown into
the world. They welcome all who come to them seeking guidance. In
an age of instant gratification this pursuit above all others deserves the
necessary time and effort. While we yearn to gain wisdom and go free, at
the same time we need patience.

FACT BOX Availability of Spiritual Knowledge

Any reasonable bookshop these days has shelves groaning under the weight of new age books on every subject from Vedantic scripture, via the chakras and wiccan spells to tarot, astrology and self help. We live in an amazing age for the availability of texts and teachings which were previously hidden away from general view in temples, ashrams, churches, mosques and synagogues. When the British arrived in India they found it, initially, impossible to convince the Brahmin pundits to part with the knowledge of Sanskrit and the sacred texts. Gradually a level of trust developed and scholars like Sir William Jones began to translate and make available some of the vast corpus of Sanskrit works. Beethoven was said to have died with a copy of the Upanishads under his pillow, Emerson treasured his copy of the Bhagavad Gita.

And today? A visit to a bookshop, a casual browse through the local library, a click on an internet link, and, hey presto! All the wisdom of the ages lies before us. We live at a time in human history when the holy grail of esoteric knowledge is available to us as never before; a time which past seekers could only have dreamed of. And yet, regardless of this unprecedented availability of the sum total of human wisdom, many of us continue to suffer from a lack of the peace and fulfilment which these works tantalisingly offer. The missing piece is to take the words of the masters and actually put them into practice.

The Seven Levels of Mankind

Let's therefore look at how mankind is organised into those who are here to learn, the outer circle of humanity, and those who are here to teach, the inner circle. The outer circle consists of ordinary people going about their ordinary affairs – going to work, looking after their families, meeting their friends, getting, spending, living, dying. This outer circle isn't just working people. It includes, princes and prelates, poets and musicians, judges on their benches, chancellors in their universities and Prime Ministers and Presidents. It includes all those who see the ordinary, mundane world of give and take as more real than the subtle world of spirit.

Some in this outer circle have a feeling that there is a higher consciousness, but lack much knowledge of how to access it freely. As Winston Churchill said of Stanley Baldwin: 'Occasionally he stumbled over the truth, but hastily picked himself up and hurried on as if nothing had happened.'[21] The outer circle has work to do, phone calls to make, nappies to change, and nations to govern. By and large the vast majority of people in the outer circle are too distracted to ask questions like Who am I? Does life have a purpose? Can anyone teach me how to go free? A man of my acquaintance, explaining his absence from a spiritual meeting, said that he had less important things to do.

This outer circle is divided into three: first, those wedded to satisfying their appetites and who find it hard to encompass the needs of others – even their own families – if their desires would be thwarted; secondly, those who have some access to feeling and faith. Their hearts are partially open and while they look after themselves, they are also concerned for their nearest and dearest. And thirdly, there are those with some access to reason and intellect who can operate on a wider sphere accommodating their community, co-religionists and countrymen.

Beyond the outer circle is an inner circle where the great teachers, prophets, masters and saints live. This inner circle is also divided into three levels: master teachers and prophets; saints and sages; and fully integrated, realised men and women. Some make themselves known to the outer circle, many do not. But they are not idle. Their meditations and prayers and rituals radiate a measure of consciousness which protects all of mankind. In a way all the great philosophical texts, scriptures of all traditions, even the art, literature and music which lifts our spirits and reminds us of a higher world, are inspired by the work of men and women of the inner circle and point the way there for those who wish to make the journey.

For example, outside a fairly small specialist academic circle many have never heard of Marsilio Ficino.

FACT BOX — **Marsilio Ficino**

Marsilio Ficino (1433–1499) was the son of the Medici family physician. Cosimo D'Medici, an astonishing man in his own right, spotted Ficino's extraordinary potential when he was still a boy. Cosimo had him educated in the classics including, unusually for those days, Greek. He then set Ficino the task of translating into Latin all the ancient Greek manuscripts which Cosimo's agents could acquire.

Ficino therefore made the first Latin translations of the complete works of Plato

---

[21] Quoted in S Hayward, *Churchill and Leadership,* Gramercy Books, New York, 2004, p. 4

and Hermes Trismegistus from Greek, making them available for the first time in two millennia to Western Europe. He became the leader and guide of a group of scholars, poets and writers known as the Platonic Academy. They met in a villa given over for that purpose by Cosimo.

Botticelli was under his guidance when he painted some of his allegorical works like *La Primavera*. He was also one of Lorenzo D'Medici's teachers, and he corresponded with princes and prelates and men of influence throughout Europe, guiding and advising them on how to live virtuously. Ficino corresponded with and inspired John Colet, the Dean of St Paul's cathedral and a friend of Sir Thomas More. John Colet in turn founded St Paul's school which, even today, is one of the finest educational institutions in the world.[22] This is the spreading influence of those in the inner circle.

Ficino died in 1499 in semi-exile at a time when Florence was in some disarray. He may have thought his life's work had come to nought. But in a quiet way his ideas of the dignity of man, and of a higher perfect Self spread throughout Western civilisation.

Between the three levels of the outer circle and the three levels of the inner circle there is an intermediate stage at level four. This level is in a transitional position which is only occupied at times of need in human history. I will cover these seven levels of mankind in more detail, and particularly the role of level four, in the chapter dealing with *sattvapati* – the fourth step on our way to freedom and happiness. **Practice 6** helps us connect with the inner circle. (See page 51.)

Genesis: The Seven Days of Creation

The first chapter of Genesis gives us a mysterious and mythic account of the creation of the universe in seven days. There are divergent views on the meaning and significance of this account. The literal interpretation holds it to be an account of seven periods of twenty-four hours. This view asserts that God first created the heaven and the earth, and He then said: 'Let

---

[22] The school of which I am Headmaster is named after John Colet because of his stature as a man of truth, insight, Platonic scholarship and concern for the education of children. And our sister school in Auckland is named after Ficino. The school in Melbourne is named after Erasmus who was a friend of Colet and an admirer of Ficino.

there be light.' And there was light. A twenty-four hour period later He got to grips with the firmament and the divided waters; and so on, until the seventh day when he could relax after a hard week's work.

The scientific secular view, on the other hand, is that this account is nonsense on stilts. How, sceptics scoff, can there be light on the first day, while the sources of light – the sun, moon and stars – are created on the fourth day? The trees, plants and grasses which are created on day three would certainly have a hard time of it without the sun. And how for that matter would the earth maintain a sunless orbit? The radically foreshortened timescale also causes them to roll their collectively disbelieving eyes.

So, according to the secular rationalist view, the entire account can be safely dismissed as a primitive and ignorant attempt to explain the inexplicable to ancient, misogynistic camel drivers and goatherds; and, more, there was probably a sinister aspect to all this, whereby a priestly cast sought to live off the labour of others by keeping them in ignorance and instilling the fear of a vengeful (and mythical) God. So, these scientists say, dusting off their hands, that's that.

I believe there is a middle way between implausible literalism, and dismissive rationalism. It is my view that, as with all mankind's heroic, mythic and time-tested stories, there are layers of meaning which repay interested, intelligent and respectful study. The account in Genesis is no exception. This account has a subtle inner meaning which parallels and gives guidance for the journey on the seven steps to freedom and happiness.

Genesis: The First Day – Let There Be Light

In the beginning God created the heaven – the invisible world; and the earth – the visible world. But the earth is 'formless and void' – it has yet to take distinct shape; hence all that follows is the creative process whereby the formless is brought into being as separate formed creatures ready to play their part. This creative process takes place through the separation and division of one thing from another and then naming them. And God does this through speech. What God says, goes: Let there be light, and there was light.

On the personal level, 'heaven' is our invisible world of mind, heart and spirit; and 'earth' is our outer form – our body and our behaviour.

When these worlds are in a state of flux (formless and void) we need some light to shine to clarify things for us, to give us insight into our true nature and ultimately to help us find our way to freedom.

Light and dark

The appearance of a teacher of wisdom either in person or through their words or followers is for us like a light shining in the darkness. One of the effects of this illumination is to divide the light from the darkness within us. The teacher's knowledge comes as an inspiring, energising revelation. But it can also highlight shortcomings. It divides our light from our darkness, so we can begin to recognise each for ourselves. It names the light Truth or Knowledge or Wisdom; and the darkness Ignorance or Selfishness or Ego, just as God called the light Day and the darkness He called Night.

This division of light and darkness is a common theme in myth, scripture and philosophy. Plato's cave has its image of prisoners in the dark cave, with a fire burning behind them throwing shadows on the wall. In one of the Vedic creation myths Hiranyagarbha, the universal golden egg from which the creatures spring forth, shines in the dark chaos.

Many of us experience an impenetrable darkness lying just below the observable mental and emotional world with which we seek to make sense of the world. Most of us need help and guidance to begin to take the journey into our own subconscious until we arrive at the well-spring of true being. This guidance comes in the form of illuminating wisdom from wise men and women.

My aim in this chapter has been to emphasise two points: first, such men and women have always existed, and exist now, and they are ready, willing and able to help; and, secondly, to receive their wisdom we need to be open and willing to follow what they have to say.

EMPTYING OUR CUP

There is a Zen story where a learned professor goes to a Zen master seeking wisdom. The master offers tea and when it is ready he begins to pour. He continues pouring until the cup is overflowing and the tea is spilling all over the table.

'Stop!' cries the professor, unable to restrain himself, 'The cup is full, no more will go in.'

'Like this cup,' replied the master, 'your mind is full of ideas, opinions and information. In order to receive Zen you must first empty your cup.'

We too need to approach the wisdom of the sages with an attitude of humility and openness. Even when their guidance seems odd or difficult to understand, the best advise is to give it a go. The result of putting it into practice with an open mind and heart will be to get you started on your journey to freedom. Consistent practice at this initial level of Good Impulse gets you to *suvicharana* – true enquiry – the second step on the way to freedom.

PRACTICE 3 ▶ ▶ ▶ ▶ ▶ ▶ ▶ ▶ ▶

Sit quietly and relax. Let the mind come to rest and equilibrium.

Reflect on a genuine question, or an issue which you would like resolved. Imagine that there *is* a universal consciousness; a source of knowledge and compassion. Throw caution to the winds for the purposes of this exercise – what have you got to lose?

Frame a question and, with a spirit of openness and a willingness to accept help, ask the question quietly in your mind, or speak it aloud. Then gently let it go. Maintain this state of open willingness for a few moments.

Sometimes an answer can come surprisingly quickly and clearly. Sometimes it takes a little time (hours, days, even weeks). Sometimes it pops into your mind or heart. Sometimes a chance phrase jumps off the page or from a snatch of conversation. And sometimes nothing appears to happen. Great. Give it another go. Rome wasn't built in a day.

PRACTICE 4 ▸ ▸ ▸ ▸ ▸ ▸ ▸ ▸ ▸

Take some time out of your usual schedule. Sit quietly and ask yourself some serious questions. What do I really want out of life? Is there a sense of something missing? What is it? Am I seeking true knowledge, wisdom, faith, a real purpose, the ability to serve others?

Buy a note book, something a little special would be helpful, and start making some notes on these reflections. Make sure you date the notes and reread them fairly soon afterwards both to remind you of their content and to give you an opportunity of filling them out if they are a bit cryptic.

PRACTICE 5 ▸ ▸ ▸ ▸ ▸ ▸ ▸ ▸ ▸

Here is a similar practice with a more devotional, imaginative element: Imagine there is someone knowledgeable and willing to help you, available to you right here and now. Resting quietly, feel their wisdom and love. Feel that they are fully open to help anyone who asks. What question or questions would you put to him or her? Reflect on these questions and then actually ask either silently in the mind and heart, or aloud as if he or she were really present. Then gently let the question go and quietly and patiently wait for an answer.

Don't worry if an answer doesn't come immediately or in a form you expect. It may be surprisingly clear and immediate, but often it shows itself sometime later, perhaps in the chance comment of someone else or in a passage or phrase we happen to read soon afterwards. Keep yourself open and receptive for an answer.

On this journey to freedom, no matter how far we go, it is always useful to ask for help.

PRACTICE 6 ➤ ➤ ➤ ➤ ➤ ➤ ➤ ➤ ➤

Reserve some time every day – ten or fifteen minutes is good – to read uplifting literature, scripture or philosophy; listen to fine music; contemplate beautiful works of art; something created by the hand of man (you can, of course, enjoy nature too, but this exercise is designed to get you into the realm of *human* wisdom).

Anything which makes you feel more calm and peaceful is what we're after: Mozart, temple chanting, Shakespeare, Khalil Gibran, some prayers or other scripture or the biographies of noble men and women are some suggestions, without wishing to dictate your choice. The key is to select something you enjoy which wakes you up rather than puts you into deeper sleep.

Gently keep returning to the present – in the Now – and try to surrender any of your own 'knowing' or preconceptions. Listen to what the masters are saying. Also don't be too watchful for uplifting results. It would be good if you simply read or listen or look, for your own rest and enjoyment, rather than as an earnest and serious pursuit.

* * * * * * *

Chapter **Two**

Step Two:
True Enquiry

CASE STUDY **ONE**

A couple are tired at the end of the day's work and when they come home various aspects of the housekeeping have been neglected. The husband shows no inclination to help; the wife feels irritated, unsupported and even unloved. A few choice words appear in her mind, which match these feelings. They are familiar words; they have been spoken before in similar circumstances.

But, she has been doing a little work on herself, on waking up, on taking control through simple exercises which have brought her back again and again to the present moment. So, this time she is aware of how, if she gives vent to her negative feelings, the situation will play out. The whole scenario is laid out before her: I'll say this; then he'll say that; then I'll say this, and so on. This awareness gives her the opportunity to apply reason. She remembers that he has also had a busy day; that he usually does get around to it eventually, but on a different timetable; she also remembers many of the other ways he contributes around the house; and she remembers that this is the man she loves, the father of her children, and she feels the love dissolve her spiky irritation.

But there is still housework to be done. So she watches the options present themselves and allows her mind to select the most appropriate one leading to the desired outcome – a tidy house and marital harmony; rather than a different outcome – a tidy house accompanied by yet another bickering, pointless argument.

When reason presents alternatives we still have to act. Reason itself is essentially passive. It merely presents the options. We then need the energy, the will, the desire to act in a reasonable way and to turn our back on an unreasonable course of action. Sometimes this is not as easy as it sounds.

CASE STUDY **TWO**

A business executive has made his way to the top of the corporate ladder with energy, drive and commitment. He is now approaching middle age, is on his third marriage and hardly ever sees his children. He sees himself as focused, attentive to detail and passionate about excellence. He won't allow himself to pushed around or treated disrespectfully. He shouts a lot. His employees are terrified of his temper and are reluctant to bring him any bad news. One day he has a sudden and clear vision of where his life is heading – a few more wives, many more deals, a lot of money and a lonely and friendless old-age – and it frightens the life out of him.

He begins to look for someone who can teach him how to find peace and happiness. By good fortune he finds a teacher and devotes his considerable energy and intelligence to putting the advice of the teacher into practice. Some of these practices are easy and have an immediate effect – he feels calmer, more awake and more in touch.

But he often blows his stack when his will is thwarted. And he still finds himself saying needlessly hurtful things to his wife and friends. He hates himself for it afterwards and this is a new feeling.

So he seeks further guidance on how to restrain cruel and abusive speech and he redoubles his efforts to work against this habitual tendency. This effort begins to pay off and after a while he finds this negative, angry speech largely becomes a thing of the past. Our friend has met and passed beyond the second step on the way to freedom.

The Prodigal Son

In the last chapter we looked at the story of the prodigal son which tells us of the whole journey of humanity from enlightenment into ignorance and back again. The first part of the story is an allegory of the descent of the soul from unified bliss (the father's house) to the hard graft of work in a world of separation and limits (the pig-pen). At the first stage of good impulse our desire to change and our willingness to follow wise guidance sets us, like the prodigal son, on the path home to freedom. At his lowest ebb the prodigal son wakes up – 'he came to himself' – and he says:

> *How many hired servants of my father's have bread enough and to spare and I perish with hunger! I will arise and go to my father, and will say unto him, 'Father, I have sinned against heaven, and before thee, and am no more worthy to be called thy son: make me as one of thy hired servants.'* [23]

This memory of his father's house is the good impulse. It gets him moving. Then he arose and began his return journey to his father's house. To complete the first step of Good Impulse this is the clincher: to do something – anything!

Suvicharana

The next step for the prodigal son, and for us, to be readmitted into our father's house, involves further action which is purposeful, intelligent and effective. Here knowledge is needed, which is why *Yoga Vasishtha* calls the second step to freedom Enquiry. This needs a little explanation. The Sanskrit name for this second step is *vicharana* or *suvicharana* – good, true or propitious enquiry.

---

[23] Luke 15:11–32.

While the acquisition of information is a part of enquiry, more is needed. We are all acquainted with people who can fill any conversational gap with intimate knowledge of all sorts of things. They may beguile an idle hour or two (or three) with anecdotes on almost any conceivable topic, including spiritual knowledge. Yet their lives may be in disarray, they might let friends down, betray lovers, or be petulant with shopkeepers; they may cheat and steal on a petty (or even grand) scale. Perhaps they blame others for the ups and downs of life – which often ensures that they repeat their mistakes again and again. All their learning and glib pronouncements seem not to have affected how they live. The real study of anything begins when it is put into practice. Enquiry without action is not *vicharana*.

True enquiry, therefore, involves not only rational investigation into this new way of living and the steps required on the journey. It includes a change in our behaviour. Some of our physical habits change – getting up a little earlier, eating better food, punctuating the day with yoga or meditative exercises. And True Enquiry also results in a change of mind and heart.

Narada and Sanatkumar

There is a striking example of this need for more than mere information in the Chandogya Upanishad where Narada, despite extensive study, asks the sage Sanatkumar to fill in the missing piece – Self-knowledge. First Narada gives Sanatkumar his impressive résumé:

> *Lord! I know Rig-Veda, Yajur-Veda, Sama-Veda, Atharwa-Veda, history and tradition called the fifth-Veda, grammar, ritual, mathematics, astrology, mineralogy, logic, economics, physics, metaphysics, zoology, politics, astronomy, mechanics, fine arts. Lord! Yet these things are but elementary knowledge; I do not know the Self. I have heard from masters that he who knows Self, goes beyond sorrow. I am lost in sorrow. Help me to go beyond.*[24]

With all his considerable learning, Narada has no experiential knowledge of the true inner Self without which one remains bound by sorrow.

---

[24] *Ten Principal Upanishads,* op. cit. p. 96ff.

True enquiry – *vicharana* – includes both information and experience leading to true understanding. Narada needed to go beyond mere accumulation of information and enquire deeply into the Self.

So let's begin some good or propitious enquiry by asking two simple questions which, if pursued persistently, are productive of great results. Who am I? and Where am I?

Who Am I?

Am I a physical body with a mysterious power to think and feel? Am I my opinions, theories and beliefs? Am I my emotional states? Am I my personality and character? Am I a combination of all of these? Am I confident and imaginative and open hearted, or am I timid and insecure and subject to fits of anger; am I cool and detached from the ups and downs of life, or passionately involved in a myriad of causes. Am I a mixture of qualities – 'all of the above' – depending on the circumstances? Am I one person in the morning and another at night? Was I someone when I was young, but am I now someone else?

Who am I? The possibilities are endless.

An example: A young woman has various facets to her character. Sometimes she is focused and passionate with a good heart and a sense of humour; but her friends and acquaintances handle her with care because, if they say or do the wrong thing, she explodes. So who is she? A lively passionate friend with an alarming capacity to blow her stack; or a human timebomb who can be quite nice sometimes?

Who am I? **See Practice 7, page 74.**

Where Am I?

Practice 7 involves getting clearer on who we believe ourselves to be. To start our journey we should also get a fix on *where* we are in time and space. Unlike the tourist asking for directions, who was told: 'If I were you, I wouldn't start from here', 'here' is the only place where we *can* start. So getting a clear idea of where we are now is essential to setting out on our journey to freedom.

So, where am I? Here and now would be a good answer – if it were true. **Practice 8 (see page 74)** is designed to help us be here and now for a few minutes. After trying this practice it may become clear to us that the first answer to the question Where am I, is generally speaking, absent. When we try to be present, we find our attention continually whipped away. A snatch of a song, a half remembered insult, an anticipated delight or dread and we are 'off with the fairies'. We see a bag, which we bought on holidays, and wouldn't it be nice to go to Tasmania, where they have Tasmanian Devils, and wasn't there one on Bugs Bunny? You get the idea.

This exercise, along with all of the others in this book, repays gentle repetition and persistence. The regular endeavour to be here and now is indescribably valuable, and will very quickly show results in greater awareness, wakefulness and control. It immeasurably aids our progress through the seven steps to freedom and happiness. This enquiry into who and where we are, and the efforts we make to be present and awake will have an immediate observable effect on us. And the more we do it the greater the effect. My own experience and that of many others who endeavour to be more aware and present is that the mind begins to settle, we feel more awake and alive, our relationships can even be warmer and happier.

And we can become aware of another aspect of our being; a part of us which is fleeting and elusive, but is still, peaceful and watchful. Later in this chapter (page 69) I will discuss this inner witnessing consciousness, and its ugly step sister – the Ego. But before doing so I must deal with one effect of deepening enquiry: inner division.

Inner Division

Before we encounter the guidance of a teacher many of us find life confusing, and our powers to understand its deeper laws weak. Our life is generally a mixture of pleasant and unpleasant experiences largely beyond our control. At this stage, before we take the first step on the way to freedom, we are pulled by the twin poles of pleasure and pain. We veer between our better impulses and our worse ones: we give to charity but shout at the kids; we are honest at work but gossip about our friends behind their back. And guilt eats at us.

Then we find an inspiring source of wisdom and we try to live another way, restraining our meaner impulses and strengthening our more positive tendencies. We try to make a change in ourselves, and the initial actions we take at step one, Good Impulse, do indeed change us. The willingness to change, and the action based on this desire, now begin to clarify our opposing tendencies – light and dark, yes and no, old and new. Our old habits continue to press their claims; and, at the same time, under the guidance of the wise, a new self, a still inner observer, begins to show itself.

Some of us feel we are slipping backwards because the advice of the teacher both inspires and energises our better parts while at the same time they throw new light on our habitual ways and other limitations in our thoughts, feelings and actions. This can (and usually does) lead to some doubts and a feeling of uncertainty. The movement away from the old negative tendencies, and in the direction of conscious control and freedom requires effort, resolve and determination guided by reason and the words and advice of a mentor. The good company of others who are also searching is essential, because it is not all plain sailing; the natural desire arises to find a group of like-minded people.

Good Company

At this point a few words on the nature of good company are needed. On this path to freedom most of us need the encouraging fellowship of others who are at a similar stage. While it strikes a slightly false note to speak of 'ahead' or 'behind' in spiritual work, nevertheless in the play of creation these concepts have a certain utility. We naturally turn to those who are ahead of us for guidance. And we also seek out those at a similar stage who can empathise with us, and with whom we can share our experiences. Some find a formal organised structure like an ashram or, in my case, the School of Philosophy. For others it seems more open and spontaneous, but whether it comes in the form of personal contact or through reading or study, good company is one of the essential requirements.

In Sanskrit good company is called *satsanga* – the meeting of the good or wise. Getting together with others on the way is important because, in the divided state at stage two, the aspirant will inevitably be assailed both from within and without by 'the thousand natural shocks that flesh is heir to'. No matter how strong you feel, these will strike at the chinks in your armour. These chinks are specifically designed by nature to test you, and by your own ego to return you to a compliant state; hence the need for a guide and for encouragement from others.

Without the good company of other seekers it is extremely difficult to make lasting progress. Here is a provocative assertion: in the company of good people it is almost impossible to act badly; in the company of bad people it is almost impossible to behave well. This is not meant to be critical or judgmental – it is simply an observable fact. Good company is therefore powerful.

So who are these good people? And what do I mean by bad people?

Good people are truthful, honest, kind, compassionate, courageous and do the right thing when it is difficult, unpopular or at personal cost; they also restrain themselves from doing the wrong thing even when it is to their advantage and when it is easy and popular. Bad people are dishonest, deceitful, cruel, selfish, cowardly and do things regardless of whether they are right or wrong if they believe they will derive some benefit or pleasure from doing so; and will hold back from doing the right thing if it is difficult or they have to sacrifice some pleasure or advantage.

From these descriptions you will see that very few of us are totally good or completely bad – we are all a bit of a mix. If we seek perfect company we may find ourselves with what a friend of mine described as 'a job with a future'. Jane Austen was aware of this:

> 'My idea of good company…is the company of clever, well-informed people, who have a great deal of conversation; that is what I call good company.'
> 'You are mistaken,' said he gently, 'that is not good company, that is the best.' (Persuasion)

So we should seek out (and will probably find ourselves drawn to) the company of those who are interested in the pursuit of higher consciousness. Not perfect people, certainly, but people who are making an honest endeavour to be better than they were, to wake up, to live a reasonable life, to speak truthfully and, most importantly, when they slip or stumble or fail, they will make concerted efforts to rectify the error and press on. This is good company.

Here is a story which illustrates the mysterious power of *satsanga*, the good company of the wise.

THE POWER OF SATSANGA

Narada, the great heavenly devotee went to see Lord Vishnu, Preserver of the Universe, and bowed low before him.

'Yes, O Narada, tell me why you have come. What do you wish of me? I cannot resist the wishes of my devotees,' said Lord Vishnu, who, knowing the secrets of all our hearts, already knew why Narada had come. Out of compassion and grace he allowed his devotee to address him with a question.

'O Great Lord of All,' said Narada, 'You know everything there is to know in the whole great universe. I have heard you extol satsanga, the company of the wise. Please, if your grace allows, tell me of the power of satsanga.'

Lord Vishnu smiled a secret smile and said, 'O Narada, this is a difficult question. Even the wise discuss and dispute over the power of satsanga. I cannot give you an immediate answer. But,' he continued, seeing the astonishment and disappointment on Narada's face, 'I can tell you who to ask. Go down to earth disguised as a man. On earth go to the plain of Kurukshetra. By the plain of Kurukshetra there grows a Tamarind tree, on that tree is a branch, and on that branch a small worm is crawling. Find that worm and ask him about the power of satsanga.'

Narada was mystified by this strange instruction but hurried to do his Lord's bidding and soon arrived at the very tamarind tree by the plain of Kurukshetra. On that tree he saw, on one of the branches a small worm slowly crawling along its length.

Narada bowed low to the worm and greeted him respectfully. 'O Worm, I wish to ask a question of you.'

'O Great Sage,' said the worm, 'What an honour it is to meet you. I will do my best but how can I, a lowly worm, possibly answer any question that you, a great and wise heavenly being, might ask me?'

Narada secretly agreed that the likelihood was slender but felt he had to follow Lord Vishnu's strange instructions. So he asked: 'O Great Worm, tell me if you are pleased to do so, what is the true power of satsanga?'

On hearing these words the worm began to shiver and shake and dropped from the branch of the tamarind tree to the plain of Kurukshetra stone, cold dead. Narada was taken aback and returned to heaven to report this extraordinary happenstance to Lord Vishnu.

'Hmm', said Lord Vishnu, the innermost ruler of all hearts, 'This is very curious. Let me think about it and we will talk again in a little while.'

A few weeks later Lord Vishnu summoned Narada and said, 'If you are still curious to know the power of satsanga, go to earth again disguised as a man and, near the plain of Kurukshetra you will find a mango tree. In that tree you will find a newly hatched parrot of beautiful plumage. Ask that parrot to tell you about the power of satsanga.'

Narada, the great devotee of Lord Vishnu, was overjoyed at this instruction and was soon standing before the mango tree. He espied the newly hatched parrot with beautiful plumage. 'O Parrot,' he said politely, 'How beautiful your plumage is.'

'Many thanks, O Narada,' said the parrot, bowing low. 'What a great honour it is to be visited by you. Can I be of service to you in any way?'

'Yes, O wise bird,' said Narada. 'Tell me if you would, about the power of satsanga, the company of the wise.'

And no sooner had Narada spoken these words than the parrot began to shiver and shake and dropped down onto the sacred soil of Kurukshetra stone cold dead.

Narada was amazed and sorry to see the beautiful parrot lying dead at his feet. He worried that his question had somehow caused the parrot to expire. He returned to heaven in a troubled frame of mind.

Vishnu again, appeared to be perplexed by this turn of events and asked Narada to give him time to reflect. Time went by and Narada busied himself with his duties of singing the praises of Vishnu and visiting holy men to bring them comfort in their spiritual endeavours.

Nearly a year went by after the death of the parrot when Narada was again summoned to the presence of Vishnu. 'O Narada, are you still eager to find out about the power of satsanga, the company of the wise sages?'

'Yes, Lord,' said Narada fervently, 'But, the question seems to have serious consequences for the hearer. Do you think it is safe to go on asking?'

'Let's find out,' said Lord Vishnu, 'Near the sacred plain of Kurukshetra there is a farm. On that farm is young calf. Go down to earth disguised as a man and go to that calf and ask him to tell you of the power of satsanga.'

Narada went immediately and found the farm. On that farm he found the young calf and he approached it with joined hands and bowed low.

'Greetings O Wise One,' said the calf, 'I am truly blessed to be visited by a sage such as you. How can I be of service?'

'O beautiful calf,' said Narada, 'Allow me to ask you a question. The great Lord Vishnu himself recommended you as one I should ask.'

'Please proceed and I will answer as best I can,' said the calf.

'Tell me, I beg you, what is the true power of satsanga, the company of a wise man?'

The calf, on hearing these words, began to shiver and shake and he dropped down dead at Narada's feet. Narada was horrified. 'I have killed a sacred cow!' he thought, 'I am accursed. I will wander the earth doing penance to cleanse myself of sin.'

And he spent several years wandering through the world serving the wise, comforting the grief stricken, teaching the inquisitive and spreading the healing balm of devotion to Vishnu across the face of the earth. Finally he returned to the abode of Vishnu and bowed low and begged forgiveness for being the cause of the death of a sacred calf. Vishnu forgave him and he was washed clean of any taint of sin.

But what of the power of satsanga? Narada hardly dared to raise the subject but Vishnu said: 'We must decide on the power of the company of the wise sages once and for all. Go down to earth just one more time. In the land bordering the sacred field of Kurukshetra there stands the palace of a righteous king and his beautiful and devoted queen. They have been blessed with a young and handsome prince who is still but a boy. Go to that young prince and ask him of the power of satsanga.'

So Narada, full of anxiety, went to earth and sought out the palace of the king. His innocent question had, it seemed, led to the death of the worm in the tree, the beautiful newly born parrot and the young calf. What would happen if he asked his question and the prince dropped dead! What a calamity would befall the kingdom. Perhaps the righteous king and queen would even curse Narada who would be bound by this curse for ages until freed by further penance and the healing grace of the Lord.

But Narada, obedient to the instructions of his God, entered the palace and asked for an audience with the King. The King and Queen, seeing Narada, eagerly vacated their thrones and bowed low in the presence of the Divine Narada.

'What a privilege it is to welcome you to our palace. How can we be of service,' said the King. And the Queen also bowed low and offered water and fruit to Narada.

'For many years I have been seeking an answer to the question about the power of satsanga. I have sought to discover the mystery of the power of the company of the wise. I put the question to Lord Vishnu himself and he has sent me to ask a worm, a parrot and a calf and now he has told me to ask your son the prince.'

The King and Queen were surprised, after all their son was only five years old. But they didn't hesitate even when Narada told them of what had happened to the others of whom he had asked the question. 'After all,' they said, 'Everyone must die. But who can earn the privilege of passing to the other world in obedience to the direct command of Lord Vishnu? Surely our son is greatly blessed whatever happens.'

So the boy was summoned, and when he entered the throne room and he saw Narada he ran to him and threw himself at his feet and said with a look of supreme bliss, 'At last, my Guru has returned to me. I have waited these five years to again sit at your feet!'

Narada was completely dumbfounded. What could this strange speech mean?

'O Prince,' he said, 'I do not understand. We have never met. I have come here, as instructed by Lord Vishnu, to ask _you_ about the power of satsanga.'

The boy laughed in complete delight and pointed at Narada and said: '_You_ are the power of satsanga!'

'Whatever can you mean,' said Narada, even more perplexed.

'It is simple,' said the Prince, 'Some years ago I was born as a worm doomed to spend innumerable births as a lowly creature, waiting to earn the right to be reborn in a higher form. Then you came along and just a few moments in your holy presence blessed me with a rebirth as a beautiful parrot. And, wonder of wonders! You came to me again and, from the cooling breeze of just a few minutes in your company, I was able to obtain my next birth as a sacred calf. And, O Joy of Joys! You came _again_ and just *a couple of words from you and I was born as a prince with this righteous King and Queen as my father and mother. And again you come to me. My heart is bursting with delight!'*

Now, at last, Narada, felt comprehension dawn, and he finally understood the wonderful power of satsanga.

Our Own Resources

Another aid, along with guidance and good company, on our new path is ourselves. We all have aspects of our character which we would rather be rid of – weaknesses, failings, regrets, and so on. But we also have talents, strengths and inner resources. Sometimes it is a little difficult to see these for ourselves and hence another reason to be in good company. Not only to bring out these good qualities but also for encouragement and an objective assessment of ourselves by sympathetic, trustworthy companions.

I have benefited enormously from the encouragement of my friends in the School of Philosophy and perhaps even more from their sometimes pointed assistance in alerting me to my shortcomings. I have learned, for example, that some see me as an example of working with fine attention (I would not have guessed this talent); others have been kind enough to point out my tendency to over-intellectualise, which I could then restrain. Still others have shown me the way to a deeper connection to a wellspring of feeling and emotion and the devotional side of spiritual work. And all of these – attention, restraint of excessive thinking, deep devotion – come from my own inner resources and were revealed to me by good company. We all have vast inner resources even if they are sometimes hidden from us. Getting a fetch on them and using them is a great help on our path to freedom and happiness.

Genesis: The Second Day –
The Divided Waters

On the first day God created light and immediately divided light from darkness. The good impulse provided to us by our mentor or guide acts like this light. It divides our favourable, harmonious tendencies from our dark, limited habits. With this inner division we move to step two – true enquiry. The account of the second day of creation can be read as an allegory of this divided condition and can give us some guidance.

*And God said, Let there be a firmament in the midst of the waters, and
let it divide the waters from the waters. And God made the firmament,
and divided the waters which were under the firmament from the waters
which were above the firmament: and it was so. And God called the
firmament Heaven. And the evening and the morning were the second
day.*[25]

Water is often symbolic of love because, like love, it cleanses and
purifies; like love it takes the shape of any container it fills in an act of
complete surrender, and yet goes free as soon as it is released. Like love it
is paradoxical: it is soft and yielding and yet can wear down the hardest
rock; it is life-giving, but can take life as well; it is gentle but, when roused
is utterly destructive. Love, like water, has both a binding quality, as it joins
people, families and nations together; but, on the other hand, it dissolves
and carries away substances such as hatred and selfishness where they can
be purified and cleansed. It is a catalyst for change but remains unaffected.

*Love knows no measure but is fervent above measure. Love feels no bur-
den, disdains no labours, would willingly do more than it can; complains
not of impossibility, because it conceives it may and can do all things. It
is able therefore to do anything and it performs and effects many things,
where he that loves not faints and lies down.*

*Love watches, and sleeping slumbers not; when weary is not tired, when
straitened is not constrained; when frightened is not disturbed; but like a
lovely flame and a torch all on fire, it mounts ever upward and securely
passes through all opposition.*[26]

The waters above symbolise our love for higher things (truth, virtue,
courage, compassion, our higher Self); and the waters below stand for
our love for the lower things (possessions, relationships, pleasure, our
opinions and cherished beliefs, our egos). This is the divided condition.
And our desire now pulls us in two opposite directions. We want the
mundane and transitory things of the world while also wanting the things
eternal – we want God *and* mammon.

---

[25] Genesis 1:6–8.

[26] Thomas à Kempis, *The Imitation of Christ* (Harold Gardner SJ, ed), Doubleday, 1955, p. 98.

The firmament makes the position clear. In the Bhagavad Gita the Prince Arjuna is in a similar position. He is on the battlefield between the forces of good and evil and he is unmanned by seeing loved ones in both camps. This is our situation at step two. We are wedded to our old habitual ways and drawn to a new higher way. And this is not necessarily a comfortable or stable condition – like water it is fluid and can be turbulent.

This may come as a surprise to some of us. After all, isn't the rise in self-knowledge meant to bring bliss, wakefulness and a sense of being grounded in reality? Yes and no. It is like the learning curve of any new study. An initial burst of success followed by some hard grind. In the dreams of the uninitiated those seeking higher consciousness should be ever serene, noble and calm; and these saintly souls should glide tranquilly through minor challenges, and most of the major ones, of life. This is rarely the case (I speak from personal experience). Spiritual advancement does not mean being free of troublesome events, disturbing thought or awkward people; rather it means meeting them effectively, reasonably and compassionately. And to do this consistently, requires practice, effort and application over time.

THE BUDDHA AND THE DOCTRINE OF GREAT LOVE

There is a story of the Buddha that illustrates that even the wise aren't free of life's challenges. The Buddha taught the doctrine of great love and compassion. A man, hearing this and thinking of his own cares and worries became incensed. It was all right, he thought, for the Buddha, surrounded by disciples who adored him and who tended to his every need, to expound such an impractical philosophy, but what about ordinary people who had to deal with the realities of life!

In fact, he was so angry that he sought out the Buddha and in a public gathering rose and began to shout and hurl abuse at him. The Buddha listened with limitless love and compassion and, when the man had finished, said: 'My son, if a man offers a gift to another, and the recipient refuses to accept it, to whom does the gift belong?'

'In that case the gift remains the property of the giver,' replied the man.

'Correct,' said the Buddha, 'I refuse to accept your gift of anger and abuse. You may keep them, and I hope that they will do you good.' The man went away ashamed, but, the story says, returned and took refuge in the Buddha.

Even the Buddha couldn't avoid being offered the 'gift' of anger and abuse. But he was able to decline the gift. One of our goals is to reach that state where we also decline the gift of anger, abuse or tragedy and disappointment. Like the Buddha, we can then meet the events of life with love and compassion. And to do that we have to find a place within ourselves – a firmament – where we can stand and observe our own higher and lower nature. **See Practice 9, page 75.**

Individuality

I started this chapter by looking at enquiry, and asking Who am I? and Where am I? I then examined the divided condition. Both these topics lead to the discussion of individuality and ego.

All of us (including the wise) have individual physical bodies with unique DNA and unique attributes such as height, weight, colouring and metabolism. Our physical bodies also have characteristic strengths and weaknesses. In the same way we all (including the wise) have unique individual natures, with a particular balance of tendencies: vigour, or compassion, or love of justice, or hatred of ignorance; and we also have our fears, hopes, irritations, desires. It is this unique blend of light and shade which gives us our distinct personality.

And this personality doesn't disappear when we start to examine and discard ignorance and move towards greater happiness and freedom. Rather this unique individual nature begins to refine. Say we are out of shape and overweight, and we decide to get our act together. We diet and exercise, and after a time we become fitter and healthier. We would still be recognisably ourselves, but we would have shed fat and toxins and have built up muscle and energy. It is the same for those parts of us beyond the physical – our emotional, mental and spiritual bodies. Many of us feel the need to go on a spiritual diet and fitness regime. The unwanted spiritual pounds come in many forms but the general term for all of them is 'ignorance'. Ignorance simply means believing something to be true which isn't (no matter how fervently we would like it to be).

And the most important form of ignorance is the belief that we ourselves are someone or something we are not. We are like a crazy man who believes he is Napoleon Bonaparte.

THE MAN WHO THOUGHT HE WAS NAPOLEON

A man walks into a psychiatrist's office dressed in a grey greatcoat with a hat turned sideways on his head. 'My name is Napoleon,' says the man.

'Oh yes,' says the psychiatrist, thinking, we've got a ripe one here. 'How can I help you.'

'Well,' says Napoleon, 'I've been having some trouble with my wife, the Empress Josephine. I worry all the time about her. She drives me crazy.'

'I see,' says the psychiatrist. 'That sounds terrible. But I think I can help. Why don't you try a little exercise of sitting still and resting in the present moment and connecting with your senses. It will make you much calmer.'

'Fine,' says Napoleon, 'That sounds good. I'll try it.' And off he goes.

He comes back a few days later looking much happier. 'That exercise was great! Josephine doesn't worry me at all any more,' he says, 'But I've got another problem. I've just invaded Russia, winter is coming and I'm really anxious.'

'Hmm,' says the psychiatrist thoughtfully, 'that does sound bad. But I think I've got something else which might help. Whenever you find yourself worrying, just turn your attention onto whatever you're doing – walking, eating, talking – and give it your full concentration.'

'Okay,' says Napoleon, 'that sounds pretty good. I'll give it a go.' And away he goes.

A few days later he comes back again looking much happier.

'You look great,' says the psychiatrist. 'Did the last exercise help?'

'Oh, yes,' says Napoleon enthusiastically, 'I hardly think about the Russian winter at all. But there is another thing which is getting me down.'

'Oh, yes?' says the psychiatrist.

'Yes,' says Napoleon, 'I have a big battle coming up against the Duke of Wellington at a place called Waterloo and it's really making me depressed. I think I'm even getting an ulcer.'

'I suppose that's why you keep your hand in your jacket,' says the psychiatrist, 'Well I happen to know a system of deep transcendental meditation which can really get you in touch with your inner self.' And, having been initiated, Napoleon goes away again.

The next time he comes back, before he can say anything, the psychiatrist says: 'Look, can I just say one thing. It's great that all these exercises are making you feel better but there is just one crucial little thing you need to know.'

'What's that?' says Napoleon.

'You're not Napoleon Bonaparte!' says the psychiatrist.

And that is the point of this story. This crazy man never was, isn't now, nor ever will be Napoleon. All the spiritual and psychological help in the world is of no real use if it just makes him a happier, better Napoleon. One day the psychiatrist, or the teacher, guru or someone, needs to tell him he is not Napoleon! He is not this false self who he believes himself to be.

And neither are we.

In some way or another we *all* think we are Napoleon. And we all have our Josephines who drive us crazy, our Russian winters which make us anxious, and our battles of Waterloo which have us tossing and turning at night. We also have our imperial coronations which delight us, our victories and triumphs which puff us up. One day however, if we are very lucky, someone will tell us – in a way which we can hear – that we are not Napoleon. And this brings us to the Ego.

The Ego

The Sanskrit term for the ego is *Ahankara*. This is a compound of *aham* and *kara*. *Aham* means 'I am' and signifies pure being, unmixed with any false identification. *Kara* means any created thing. *Kara* is derived from the root form *kri* which is the basis of all words to do with activity and creativity. Our old friend *karma* is one of its derivations and in fact the English word *create* and all its related words also comes from this root. While *aham* – 'I am' – standing for pure being, is eternal; *kara* – anything created – has a beginning and therefore must have an end. So *ahankara* literally means 'I am something'.

Ego – *ahankara* – is therefore the false identification of pure, limitless being with something, anything, of the limited creation. The underlying message of the ego is: 'I – the limitless, pure consciousness – am identified with, and believe myself to be some limited, finite, created thing subject to birth and death.'

This identification is spoken into existence and maintained when we say to ourselves: I am this body of mine, I am tall, short, fat, thin, beautiful, ugly; I am my thoughts and opinions, I am bright, dumb, clever, stupid, insightful, flummoxed; I am kind, cruel, sensitive, isolated; I am what I do, I am a mother, lawyer, tennis player; I am my feelings, I am happy, sad, irritated, depressed. We could make an endless inventory of these identifications – body, mind, job, family, feelings, ideas, ideology, beliefs, friends, enemies, needs, stresses and strains, delights and pleasures.

One of the 'Alice Through the Looking Glass' effects of the ego which keeps us in thrall to its veils of illusion is that it makes the eternal, limitless, universal Self appear tentative, ephemeral and elusive like a spiritual will o' the wisp. And it makes that which is temporary, ever-changing and subject to birth and death – like our physical body – seems solid, dependable and real. So, one simple means of attaining freedom is to use reason to sift the transient from the eternal; to detach from the transient; and to identify with the eternal.

The Snake and the Rope

Why we, the limitless, identify with the transient is one of the profound mysteries of the universe. There is no real answer to this question. A useful and oft repeated analogy is the snake and the rope. Imagine you are in the countryside at dusk and you are walking along a path. Suddenly you see a snake lying across the path. Your heart races and you are close to panic. All sorts of thoughts and fears assail you and you are frozen in terror. Then you bring your torch to bear on the snake and discover to your immense relief that it is in fact a piece of old rope casually and carelessly discarded.

Asking how the limitless can become identified with the limited is like asking how the rope magically turned itself into a snake. And asking how we can go free of our ignorance and become enlightened is like asking how we can turn the snake back into a rope. We can't. It never was a snake. But it sure gave us a fright! The key element in the story is the torch. Shining light on our situation moment by moment; resisting the urge to see it as a process but just waking up here and now, again and again is the key.

WAKE UP

There is a story of a young man who wished to test a Rabbi who was famed for his wisdom.

'Just say I am having a dream,' asked the young man, 'where I am on a ship which begins to sink. I am with my older brother and my younger sister and I can only save one of them. What should I do?'

'Wake up,' replied the Rabbi. [27]

Separating *Aham* from *Kara*

For now, rather than ask how or why egoic ignorance began, let's ask how it might end. This mirage-like ignorance is in the Vedic tradition grouped under five headings: identification with the physical body, with our function in life, with mind, with the intellect, and with happiness. And these five identifications act like sheathes, veiling our sight from the truth of who we are.

Some make the mistake of thinking the things identified with have to be dissolved, banished, even destroyed. But true freedom lies simply in placing *aham* and *kara* in their proper sphere without denying either. We should note here that all the things which are associated with body, life, mind and so on – tallness, insight, stupidity or delight – exist. But the idea that you are these things is the problem. Freedom lies in dissolving the *false* identification of *aham* – I am – with these sheathes of illusion. Then we experience pure unalloyed being, while at the same time fully enjoying the *kara* – everything presented by the universe. This is one of the esoteric meanings of the seventh commandment, 'Thou shalt not commit adultery'. It cautions us against identifying *aham* with *kara* which is a sort of adulteration of two unlike things.

Take the basic idea that I am my body. We have a wonderful, complex physical body which breathes, digests food, and performs an infinite number of minute functions throughout the day to keep its temperature constant, its systems free of disease, its cells nourished and oxygenated and so on. It is a truly miraculous machine but, and here is the key point, we

---

[27] S Sheinkin, *Rabbi Harvey Rides Again,* Jewish Lights Publishing, Vermont, 2008, p. 59.

are not our body. When through practice on the way to complete freedom we realise this we experience a great sense of freedom and joy and have a strong sense of ourselves as the steady, peaceful witnessing consciousness. When this realisation dawns the physical body doesn't disappear in a puff of smoke. It still carries us around and acts as a portal of interaction with the universe via the senses. It still needs to be fed, clothed and exercised and put to bed at night. But knowing that we are not the body, we can see it for what it is – a fine instrument ready to do our will and needing our care – while we rest in the knowledge of who we really are.

The mixing of *aham* and *kara* is a logical impossibility, because 'I am' – pure being – is the ultimate observer; and the things of the creation – *kara* – including our bodies, thoughts, feelings and even the subtle sense of our existence are all capable of being observed. Observation needs a space between the observer and the observed, so we cannot be that which we can observe.

The aim of the seven steps to freedom and happiness is to realise our true Self to be the ultimate observer – conscious, aware, awake and attentive. We will now have a closer look at this observer. After all, if we intend to set out on a journey it is good to know the destination. **See Practice 10, page 75.**

Being the Observer

The separation of *aham* and *kara* comes about by remembering that we are the conscious witnessing observer, rather than that which we observe. Experiencing this as often as we can, and especially in moments of excitement, stress or challenge, is an extremely powerful exercise.

A couple of warnings: first, this observer may initially seem fleeting and ephemeral, but gradually the sense of the presence of this Self strengthens. Second warning: some seekers try to appear still and merely witnessing while still subject to masses of inner movement and turmoil. The Bhagavad Gita has some hard words to say on this:

> *He who remains motionless, refusing to act, but all the while brooding over sensuous objects, that deluded soul is simply a hypocrite.'* [28]

---

[28] Sri Purohit Swami, op. cit. p. 28.

The advice is to live normally – eat breakfast, take the kids to school, do your tax returns – while simultaneously deepening your enquiry into spiritual truth. While for some (Lester Levenson, John Wren-Lewis) ignorance vanishes almost instantly, for most of us the awareness of our indwelling Self as a silent, unchanging, witnessing observer is revealed gradually as the layers of illusion are removed. It is not the observing Self which we need to create, but the false ego which needs to be dissolved.

Reason

The final aspect of *vicharana* is reason. This is the key to successfully overcoming the challenges, such as ego and desire and habits, which pop up to deflect us.

What is reason? Ultimately it is the clear-eyed vision of the truth; it is the faculty of the mind which can look objectively at things and sift out the true, useful, propitious and helpful aspects of a situation from the false, muddy, useless and harmful aspects. Remember the first case study about the bickering couple where the wife allowed reason to show a better way. She saw both paths and chose the reasonable one. **See Practice 11, page 76.**

Summary

To summarise this stage: Having found a guide, we need to enquire into his recommendations, and this enquiry involves not only study and reading but also practical application of that wisdom. A good start is to ask, 'Who am I?' and 'Where am I?' Pursuing these sorts of questions deepens *vicharana* – true enquiry. The more we practice and study, the deeper grows the rift between our ego, our old self with its ingrained, habitual ways, and our growing awareness of a conscious inner Self. The ego, or in Sanskrit *ahankara,* is the false identification of 'I am' – pure eternal being – with something of the ever changing and transient creation. Sifting the transient from the eternal is the key to freedom.

So, having engaged with true enquiry, having met some turbulence as ego comes under the light, and having stuck it out with courage and patience and above all the practical application of reason, we can now move on to the third step in our journey.

PRACTICE 7 ➤ ➤ ➤ ➤ ➤ ➤ ➤ ➤

Sitting quietly and still, focus gently on the breathing until your mind settles. Then ask yourself the question: 'Who am I now?' And gently let the question go. Allow your intelligence to settle on your body, the energies and sensations within the body, your thoughts and feelings, and your sense of individual existence. Ask the question a few times and allow any answer to come up.

Sometimes in exercises such as this we connect directly (and surprisingly) with a sense of the limitless. But it would also be good to get a fetch on who we *believe* ourselves to be in a work-a-day sense. Try therefore to let go of idealised answers along the lines of 'limitless consciousness', 'pure awareness', 'universal being' and so on. Many of us have done a little too much reading and study in this area and these sorts of answers can block progress. While they are, of course, true, we have to start from what we actually experience – the limited self who we believe and feel ourselves to be.

Having rested with this honest assessment of yourself write down a few notes on this person – strengths and weaknesses; hopes and achievements as well as fears and failures. This exercise is not meant to be depressing, just honest and clear.

PRACTICE 8 ➤ ➤ ➤ ➤ ➤ ➤ ➤ ➤

Sitting quietly and still, connect with the breathing until the mind settles. Then gently connect with each of the senses in turn. Feel the weight of your body in the chair. Feel the warmth and movement of the various energies in your body – the breath, the heartbeat, for example. When this is reasonably well established connect with sight; then taste and smell; and finally rest with the listening. Try to hear each sound and then hear all sounds as if they were one sound.

This simple connection to the senses brings you into the present moment. If thoughts or dreams take you away gently return to your body in the chair, and then reconnect with the listening. Try to hold this gentle awareness in the present for a few minutes.

In your journal make a few brief notes under two headings: the experiences related to how you feel when centred in the present; and the distractions which took you away. Both observations are useful.

PRACTICE 9 ➤ ➤ ➤ ➤ ➤ ➤ ➤ ➤ ➤

This practice lets us stand aside from our better and worse parts, watching them both. It may require a few repetitions; the idea is to get a sense of ourselves as the witnessing Self.

Take a piece of note paper and write your name as the heading. Leave a few lines of space under your name. Then below this divide the paper vertically into two columns. Head the left hand column '+' and the right hand column '−'. List all your positive attributes on the left, and all your negative tendencies on the right (assume no one except you will ever see this piece of paper, so you can be completely honest). Interestingly people with a reasonably upbeat self-image will tend to have a longer left hand column and vice versa.

Now sitting quietly and still, focus gently on the breathing until the mind settles. Feel the presence of both the positive and negative qualities without becoming enmeshed in either. Just rest, as it were between the two. Then ask yourself the question: 'What have I experienced of a Self which is beyond all these positive and negative qualities? Which watches and knows these qualities but is not affected by them?'

And gently let the question go. In the space under your name write down anything which presents itself about this quiet watching Self, no matter how tenuous or vague it seems.

PRACTICE 10 ➤ ➤ ➤ ➤ ➤ ➤ ➤ ➤ ➤

Sit quietly and still and go through the steps in **Practice 8** (page 74) where you connect one at a time with the senses and then rest in silent awareness with your eyes closed. When you are established in this state of wakeful observation ask yourself: 'Am I aware now?'

The answer is clearly yes.

Wait a few moments then ask: 'Who am I?' Don't expect or need a verbalised answer. The answer is in the feeling of being the awareness rather than the objects, thoughts and feelings of which you are aware and which you can observe.

PRACTICE 11 ➤ ➤ ➤ ➤ ➤ ➤ ➤ ➤ ➤

In a quiet moment think of a situation at home, or work or in social settings where hasty speech causes upset or chaos. Decide on just one area to work on (some of us want to build Rome in a day). It would be good if it is one which comes up regularly. Make a resolution that you will make strenuous efforts to wait a few moments before you speak or act.

When the moment comes, act on your resolution as often as possible. Wait, watch and when reason presents options go with the best available. Sometimes the best option is not to speak at all! If you forget don't worry; simply renew your resolve and try again.

• • • • • • •

Chapter **Three**

Step Three:
Refinement of the Mind

CASE STUDY **ONE**

A teenage girl, still at high school, has been involved with a meditation and yoga group for a few years. Initially she went along because her parents joined up and she liked the people and especially the nice food. As the years have passed she has developed a real interest. She has had a few experiences of peace and limitlessness. She has also had moments when it was uncomfortable, when she had to confront some spiteful tendency or selfishness in herself.

She has gained a measure of self-control and she has become conscious of the fact that many of her friends seem unable to control themselves in the same way. While they are basically decent girls they often bicker and gossip and criticise each other. Sometimes she finds herself joining in the back-biting and gossip but she regrets it afterwards and if necessary apologises later.

And worse, they do stupid things again and again without seeming to learn from experience. They take up with boys who anyone could see want only one thing and who break their hearts; most drink too much at parties and a few have even tried drugs. Our friend finds her interest in these things is minimal and often she is the one they turn to for help and comfort.

Tanumanasa

The third step on the way to freedom and happiness is *tanumanasa* which is the purification of the mind. *Tanumanasa* is a compound of *tanu* – thinning, attenuation; and *manasa,* – of the mind. *Tanu* is derived from the root form *tan* meaning thin, starved, emaciated, extended and diffuse. (It gives us English words like tenuous and attenuated.) 'Starved' and 'emaciated' may seem disconcerting concepts; but here *tanu* means starving the negative aspects of our minds which we would rather be free of: confusion, jealousy, self-criticism, or just that brainless pop song which you can't get out of your head. At this stage the negative thoughts and feelings in the mind are the enemy, and *tanumanasa* is the attenuation or thinning out of this mental clutter and negativity. This process of purification leads to increasing clarity of the mind; and this clarity and efficiency comes about through the starvation of the useless debilitating activities of the mind, and the strengthening and feeding of the focused and ordered mental functions.

By doing our best to follow the advice of our mentor at the first stage of good impulse (*shubhech-cha*); and by making efforts to stave off the challenges of ego through the use of reason and good company at stage two of true enquiry (*suvicharana*), we come to the third stage of *tanumanasa*. Now we begin to see and transcend mental clutter and we experience a growing lightness of being as some of the spiritual toxins begin to release us from their grip. *Tanumansa* therefore means 'refinement or purification of the mind'.

Genesis: The Third Day – Dry Land

In Genesis we hear that, on the third day of creation, God gathers the waters under the heaven into one place and commands the dry land to appear. He calls the waters Sea, and dry land Earth; and then commands the earth to bring forth 'grass, the herb yielding seed, and the fruit tree yielding fruit after his kind, whose seed is in itself.'[29]

At *tanumanasa* we have arrived at a certain stability where the turbulence of the second stage recedes – we have some 'dry land' on which to

---

[29] Genesis 1:9–13.

take a stand. And the results of our work so far, like plants, begin to show themselves and bear fruit. In Genesis these plants are set out in sequence: first, grass – comforting to walk on but lacking in nutrition; secondly herb yielding seed such as wheat and other grains – useful and nutritious but requiring more work in harvesting, threshing, grinding and baking, to make food; and thirdly, fruit from trees which are ready to eat and require no further effort.

At *tanumanasa* we are still surrounded by the turbulent lower waters – which stand for our earthly desires – but we are able to stand back from them on the dry land created by our previous efforts. In addition we are now beginning to see some of the fruits of our work. These show themselves in various forms. Some, such as mere information, are like grass which may be comforting but don't do much for us. Others, such as a system of discipline or restraint, are like wheat – more nutritious but needing to be applied conscientiously to be of use. And still others, such as good company or meditation, are like fruit which is inherently nourishing.

The Mind

The work at this stage of *tanumanasa* is largely mental and reflective, and involves the further use of reason and discrimination. The mind has superb faculties of interpretation, intellect and creativity, designed to analyse, decide and discriminate between the useful and the useless. Our success on the road to freedom requires a mind which is healthy, robust and well fed, so I will spend some time in this chapter looking at the mind. In doing so we will see which parts of it need to have the starvation diet, and which need to be fed and kept fit.

These two processes – starvation of the useless, and feeding of the useful parts of the mind – are related. The purification or refinement of the mind comes about by discarding the chatter, identifications, fears, dreams, anticipations and regrets which clutter the mind and render us powerless to control our lives. This purification leads to greater control, mental clarity and increased intelligence. If we jettison the clutter, the clear efficient functioning of the mind reveals itself. This basic fact seems to take some getting used to because we want to 'do' something, when it is the undoing which is needed. The wise keep telling us that we are already pure, perfect and complete; that we just have to stop believing that we are impure, flawed and limited. We don't acquire perfection; we already have it. This perfection is revealed when we stop telling ourselves we are imperfect.

But there's more. It is not just our negative ideas but also the positive ones which need to go.

The isle is full of noises

We would all like to be rid of fear, doubt and annoying mental confusion. But pleasant and familiar ideas and beliefs need to be jettisoned as well. This can be a problem because some of us cling fiercely to our treasured opinions, our secret desires, and our quiet dreams for a glorious future. Many also can't seem to let go of secret fears, righteous indignation, offended pride, even the malicious pleasure we get from twisting the knife – sometimes we just want to bang our spoons on our highchairs. These aspects of the mind are beguiling and attractive. They give us a kick and make us feel alive. In *The Tempest* Caliban, who symbolises ignorance and identification with the physical world, describes this alluring – and noisy – aspect of the 'isle' of the mind:

> *Be not afeard; the isle is full of noises,*
> *Sounds and sweet airs, that give delight and hurt not.*
> *Sometimes a thousand twangling instruments*
> *Will hum about mine ears, and sometime voices*
> *That, if I then had waked after long sleep,*
> *Will make me sleep again: and then, in dreaming,*
> *The clouds methought would open and show riches*
> *Ready to drop upon me that, when I waked,*
> *I cried to dream again.*[30]

This entrancing mental music lulls us into sleep, so that if like Caliban we wake, we cry to dream again. At this stage in our journey the temptation to sleep is ever present. *The Odyssey* is a story of the journey through the perils of the world to ultimate freedom. On the way home Odysseus

---

[30] William Shakespeare, *The Tempest,* act 3, scene 2.

and his companions came to the Land of the Lotus Eaters, and some of them ate the lotus fruit. They fell into a torpor, and when others tried to awaken them from their sleepy languor they said (according to Tennyson):

> *Surely, surely, slumber is more sweet than toil, the shore*
> *Than labour in the deep mid-ocean, wind and wave and oar;*
> *Oh, rest ye, brother mariners, we will not wander more.*[31]

There are many stories of earnest seekers being similarly beguiled by sleep and losing their way. To avoid this pitfall we need the strength built up though good impulse and true enquiry to examine and discard both the troublesome and the enthralling aspects of the mental clutter.

Surrending the Pleasant

But now another question might arise: Why should I give up the nice thoughts, the pleasant dreams, the attractive imaginings, the memories of past glories, or the hopes for a successful future? Surely I only need to get rid of the negative thoughts and feelings. Of course, these pleasant thoughts and feelings do make me a little dreamy; yes, I drive from one place to another and have no idea how I got there; yes, yes, I occasionally bump into things and forget where I put my car keys; but is this so bad? I want to be free of green-eyed jealousy, burning anger, debilitating self-criticism and that leaden sense of worthlessness which seems to lurk behind the brassy, up-beat face I present to the world; but can't I keep the nice stuff?

Sorry, no.

Here is why: these dreams – both pleasant and unpleasant – are not true, and they cut us off from what is actually going on in the Now. Regardless of how desirable were the green fields and flowing streams of the Land of the Lotus Eaters, the fact was that Odysseus's men were far from home, they had a journey to complete, companions who depended on them and families awaiting their return.

In the example of the unaware driver, regardless of how pleasant the dream, the fact is we are oblivious of reality. And if he were to say: 'So

---

[31] Alfred, Lord Tennyson, 'The Lotos-Eaters'.

what, I have driven that way a thousand times and could (and do) drive it in my sleep,' the second reason for making efforts is that we need to practise being present in these innocuous non-emergency situations so that we can be awake and present when it's challenging, and perhaps essential; when we need to care for the sick, feed the hungry, or simply remember ourselves when, in the middle of a heated argument, we are about to say something irrevocably stupid (again).

If we don't practise waking up in the easy, non-threatening times, the chances of us waking up when we need to are reduced. It is like a concert pianist who wishes to perform perfectly for her audience who has to practise her scales day after day. In a way it is a test of our sincerity. If we want the kingdom we have to pass through all seven gates and not dally along the way. We trade limitless bliss and universal knowledge for a passing dream about a new car, a large bank account or a new romance. Our success in purifying our mind is determined by our commitment to repeatedly waking up from this field of dreams. And the measure of our readiness in time of need is determined by our commitment and integrity when we are, as it were, left to our own devices. As they say: character is what you do when no one is looking. Similarly, wakefulness depends on the efforts we make when we don't appear to need them.

Practise When You Remember

But rather than get overly concerned about making these efforts when circumstances are easy or hard; mundane or special; we should just note that the real time to wake up is simply when we remember. Say you are at home, washing up, or out in the garage, or sorting the shopping; and it comes to mind to take a moment or two to sit quietly and connect with the senses, the breathing and the present moment. Assuming no crucial activity (bathing the baby or cooking a soufflé) will suffer, the strong advice is to leave what you are doing and sit and rest.

The exercises in this book or any others can only be done when you remember; and these moments of memory are pure gold. If you get into the habit of practising waking up and being in the Now when the memory presents itself, then memory itself is strengthened. It is a virtuous circle: the more you respond to the promptings of memory, the more memory will arise.

If, on the other hand, you persist in ignoring memory, then a layer of forgetfulness begins to lay itself down. When starting out on this way with the School of Philosophy we were introduced to a simple awareness exercise, outlined earlier in this book (**Practice 8, page 74**), where we were asked to sit quietly and connect with the senses and then to rest in the awareness of the present moment for a minute or two – a beautiful and very powerful exercise. Sometimes it would come to mind to do it when it was mildly inconvenient – at the sink washing the dishes or reading a book. And I would say to myself: 'I'll do it a minute when I've finished this.' Naturally the practice rarely took place and often I wouldn't remember until days later. But when I realised the trap and responded to the memory I found I remembered more and more often. There are illustrations of forgetfulness from myths and legends when a protagonist is cursed to forget something crucial at the critical time. One such story comes from the *Mahabharata*.

KARNA

Karna was the son of the Sun God and, although noble and a brilliant warrior, through misguided loyalty he allied himself to the forces of evil. As the great battle between the forces of good and evil approached, Karna went to obtain the secret of divine weapons from Parashurama, a priest who had vowed never to impart these secrets to a member of the warrior class. Karna therefore disguised himself as a brahmana, a priest, and became Parashurama's disciple and served him devotedly.

One day Parashurama felt tired. So Karna sat cross-legged and Parashurama rested with his head on Karna's leg. Karna sat very still so as not to disturb Parashurama's sleep. A poisonous worm crawled up to Karna and began burrowing into his leg and warm blood flowed onto the ground. Karna, being a warrior, sat unmoving despite his agony. The smell of the blood awoke Parashurama, who realised that only a warrior would have been able to resist the pain. He was angry at having been deceived but, as Karna had served him faithfully, he gave him the secret mantras to unleash the divine weapons. But Parashurama cursed him to forget these mantras at the moment when he needed them most.

We all sometimes seem to be under this sort of curse, where we forget the knowledge we have painstakingly acquired just when we need it most. Practising and applying the knowledge in good times and in challenging times naturalises this knowledge and makes its application instinctive so we don't then forget it in the heat of the moment. A few years ago it became clear to me that I was not really using the knowledge I had acquired in all my years of meditation and study in times of stress, anxiety or challenge. In these circumstances I would instinctively resort to old ways – worry, panic or other habitual responses. Some of which seemed to work, others didn't, but the key point is I didn't resort to inner memory of limitless consciousness. I didn't retain inner peace and integrity in the face of these confrontations. I realised that being calm and peaceful and attentive in the good times would only take me so far and I made a decision that I was going to use what I knew in times of stress.

Recently I had to phone a disgruntled parent and I found the usual reluctance arise in my heart and mind. I could have made that phone call stoically and courageously but I dismissed that option, and resolved to rest in the awareness of my inner, blissful Self and enjoy, delight in and love making the call. The conversation was open, free and harmonious (and honest). But even if it hadn't been, even if the parent had been abusive and angry (he wasn't), the resolve was still to retain the peace and love of limitless consciousness.

Encouragement

Experiences of higher states of consciousness encourage us and strengthen our resolve to wake up. By the time we begin to experience *tanumanasa* – the thinning out of mental clutter – we will have had clear, if perhaps fleeting, experiences of a deeper essence. These glimpses are pointers to a well-spring of pure consciousness which, with systematic effort, we can come to know and realise as our true Self. These experiences encourage us to press on even when the forces of ignorance appear powerful. They give us the confidence that the goal of unified bliss described by the wise does exist. The dreamlike nature of surface reality loses its appeal for us, and so we make further efforts to wake up. While the dreams weave a false picture of ourselves as limited and flawed, the experience of peace, freedom and expansion gives us a foretaste of the realisation of a true Self.

The Geography of the Mind

At *tanumanasa* there is a rising sense of inner power, particularly the power to face our own weaknesses and work with and through them to allow our true strength to show itself. And we deepen our awareness of the mental realm which previously was largely hidden from us. Some basic information about the inner geography of the mind will help give us some signposts.

The simplest division of the mind is into a part which is observable – thoughts, feelings, chatter, ideas – which we call the conscious mind; and a part which we seem at present unable to observe – our deeper identifications, sentences and hidden tendencies – which we can call the unconscious mind.

Western psychology has made great strides in mapping the various aspects of the mental or subtle world. From Freud with his threefold construct of ego, superego and id, to today's myriad of competing schools of psychology, the endeavour has been to create a meaningful framework to the understanding of the mind; to give a name and shape to that part of us which is, by definition, beyond the perception of the physical senses.

Before the advent of psychology, the Christian approach to this subtle realm involved the personification of mental forces into an elaborate and at times alarming array of angels and demons, incubi and succubi, cherubim and seraphim which visited men and played upon their soul (Greek: *psyche*). Some major insights into the inner mental realm were achieved through this doctrine, and the whole system had a generally useful tendency to objectify and depersonalise mental phenomena. But the fear of possession and the resultant excesses and witch hunts are all too well known. These persecutions sought to free a suffering soul from the torment of these forces through torture and even death. Not a palatable prospect in the early years of the twenty-first (or any other) century.

And psychology also, while giving incomparable insights and help to the afflicted, sometimes led us down the dark alleys of lobotomies, electro-shock therapy; and the mechanistic, soul-denying ideas of BF Skinner with his rats-in-a-box approach to life.

The traditional Vedic view is akin to modern psychology: it systematises the various functions of the mind under different headings; and it is also akin to the earlier approach in that these functions are often personified as gods and goddesses. In the next part of this chapter I will set out the Vedic framework in order to identify and clarify the various functions of the mental world; and, by way of illustration, we will also have a look at their mythic representations.

Antahkarana

The Sanskrit term for the mind is *antahkarana* which means 'inner' – *antah* – and 'organ' – *karana*. The mind is that area of our being which is not perceptible by the outgoing senses, but which receives and deals with the input from the senses. It is a singularity but, for ease of understanding, the Vedic tradition divides the mind into four areas or functions. These are: *manas, buddhi, chitta* and *ahankara.*

Manas – discursive mind

Manas is the interpretive discursive aspect of mind. It is 'the faculty or instrument through which thoughts enter or by which objects of sense affect the soul.'[32] The word *manas* is derived from the root form *man* meaning to think, believe, imagine, suppose, conjecture and so on. Also derived from the root *man* is the English word 'Man', which literally means 'he who thinks'. Our defining characteristic among all the creatures, therefore, is that we think.

This aspect of mind stands at the interface between the outer world of the senses and the inner world of memory and intellect. It interprets and translates external perceptible experience to the inner organs of discrimination and cognition; and it also translates memories and decisions into manifest speech and action. As *manas* is the discursive mind, it is quick and lively. It takes sense impressions and weaves pictures, words and dreams; it creates a myriad of shifting, sometimes contradictory feelings: desire, aversion, deliberation, doubt, faith, lack of faith, resolution, irresolution, patience, impatience, shame and fear.

Manas is the most obvious part of the mind because we can hear it speak and see the mental images it produces. Working well *manas*

---

[32] M Monier-Williams, A *Sanskrit-English Dictionary,* OUP, Oxford, 1979, p. 783.

receives physical sense impressions and packages them for the intellect to consider; and it takes our responses to these impressions and packages *them* into appropriate speech or action. When it is not connected to present reality, however, *manas* uses past impressions to create mayhem by weaving unreality into dreams, false opinions and the tyranny of ego leading to ham-fisted action, hasty speech and missed opportunities. Connecting *manas* to the present moment is crucial to our connection with reality.

The subtle senses

The physical senses bring in sights, sounds, and so on, and *manas's* proper function is to be ready to receive them. But it doesn't always do its job. These physical senses of sight, hearing and so on have subtle mental counterparts. Try a little experiment: recall a song and listen to it in your mind. You can hear it without having to sing it aloud or use your CD player. It is the same with sight, we can all visualise people and things in our mind. This is so common that we never question the strange fact that we can see an image of our mother and hear her voice without her being here.

The other senses: taste, smell and touch have less obvious subtle forms, which show themselves as a sort of intuition – we get a *feel* for a situation; we can *smell* a rat; we get in *touch* with our feelings; and some things leave a bad *taste* in our mouth. Sometimes these are merely the impositions of our own attitudes and identifications on the situation; but often these subtle senses give us surprising insight. To test the veracity of these intuitions a general rule of thumb is this: if the insight is divisive or negative or leads to criticism of the situation or people, then take it with a grain of salt. If it is unifying and uplifting or leads to compassion and sympathy for the frailties of others you may well be onto something.

Manas connected to the senses

Manas works properly when it accurately receives incoming sense impressions. The nervous system of the body converts sounds, sights, touches, smells and tastes into bio-electrical impulses which travel along the nerves to receptors, mainly in the brain, triggering glandular or hormonal reaction.

But how does a set of bio-electrical and glandular stimuli become Jim, or that guy we went to school with, or the smell of an apple, which we love, or broccoli, which we hate, or a song whose words we can't quite remember, or anything which we put a name and form to in our mind's eye? It is *manas* performing its function as the interpreter of physical sense impressions. It collects impressions from five senses at once, shapes them and passes them to the next organ of mind: the *buddhi*, intellect, where they can be evaluated and decisions can be made. Then a response arises from *chitta*, the storehouse of our past experiences, and we can swing into action – catch the ball, say hello, kiss our spouse, or duck behind our newspaper to avoid poor old Jim.

But when we are not in the present moment this connection to the outside world is broken, and *manas* uses its creative powers, and the *subtle* senses, to create mental images, weave dreams, replay snatches of half heard conversations and to talk incessantly. It becomes the servant of ego and this puts us into a deeper sleep, and allows the ego to rule our lives.

The physical senses are still doing their job: sounds, for example, still arrive by compression waves through the air to the ear where they are channelled up the ear canal to the ear drum moving the hammer, anvil and stirrup bones, which in turn move the fluid in the semi-circular canals, and the fine cilii in the cochlea. These then fire off those bio-electrical signals to the brain. And while all this is happening *manas* and the subtle senses are presenting us with the millionth rerun of a conversation with the boss, the wife, the husband, the children, the mother-in-law – take your pick – and we seethe away resentfully over what they said or did yesterday (or last week [or last year {or ten years ago}]); or perhaps we are planning a holiday to Bermuda. Those hapless cilii and all their auricular chums are working constantly but, when the message arrives, there is a sign on the door saying; 'Out to lunch. Not back any time soon.'

While *manas* should be presenting accurate information to the intellect, it is freewheeling, using the subtle senses to weave a sticky, binding dream to beguile us. Rumi describes this hypnotic activity of *manas*: 'And if any drowsy one should jump up from their slumber, he, the nurse Imagination, beguiles saying: "Go to sleep my darling. I won't allow anyone to disturb thy slumber".' This nurse is the disconnected *manas*. And the reason we *should* wake up is that we are lost in dreams while real life is passing us by. And these dreams usually turn into nightmares. They are always based on images of the past or future. We wallow in nostalgia for a happy past or seethe over remembered injuries, are stricken with guilt over past crimes, or we anticipate prospective triumphs or we are paralysed with fear about an imagined future. These positive and negative responses to the past and future can be summarised in Table 2:

TABLE 2:
Positive and negative responses to the past and future

	Past	Future
Positive	Nostalgia, pleasant memories; reliving past glories.	Hopes, pleasant anticipations.
Negative	Shame, guilt at our own past wrongs; regret at missed opportunities; resentment at past wrongs done to us.	Anxiety, fear.

To be free of the negative we need also to relinquish the positive – if you want nostalgia you will get guilt; anticipation slides seamlessly into anxiety. Giving up both frees us from fear and regret. And to do this we make continuous efforts to connect to the physical senses in the present moment. Rumi went on to say, 'But you, if you are wise, will tear up your sleep by the roots. Like the thirsty man who has heard the sound of running water.'

Indra and the ants

Manas is personified in Vedic mythology as Indra, the king of the lesser gods; in Greek and Roman mythology, *manas* is Hermes or Mercury, the crafty and sometimes impish swift-footed messenger of the gods. Indra can be wilful, and he and his godly forces are often defeated by the demons and cast out of heaven. Usually an appeal to one of the three great gods, Brahma, Vishnu or Shiva, restores the balance and a chastened Indra once more takes his rightful place on the throne of heaven. These stories illustrate the waywardness of *manas* and the need to keep it under control.

INDRA AND THE ANTS

After defeating the demon Vritra, Indra was elevated to the rank of King of the Gods, and he ordered Vishvakarma, the heavenly craftsman, to build him a grand palace. Indra was full of pride and Vishvakarma became irritated and tired as Indra asked for more and more changes and additions and improvements. Finally Vishvakarma appealed to Vishnu, the Preserver, for help. Vishnu disguised himself as a boy priest and visited Indra's lovely new palace.

As is fitting when visited by a member of the priestly caste Indra welcomed the boy and showed him around. The boy was impressed and praised Indra's palace. He added that none of the previous Indras had such a palace. At first, Indra was amused by the brahmin boy's claim to know of former Indras. But the amusement turned to dismay as the boy talked about Indra's ancestors, about the great cycles of creation and destruction, and of the infinite number of worlds scattered through the void, each with its own Indra. The boy claimed to have seen them all.

During the boy's speech, a procession of ants entered the hall. Seeing the ants the boy laughed. Meekly, Indra asked the boy why he was laughing. The boy revealed that the ants were all former Indras.

Another visitor entered the hall. He was Shiva, in the form of a hermit. On his chest lay a circular cluster of hairs, intact at the circumference but with a gap in the middle. Shiva revealed that each of these chest hairs corresponded to the life of one Indra. Each time a hair fell, one Indra died and another replaced him.

Feeling humbled Indra was no longer interested in wealth and honour. He rewarded Vishvakarma and released him from any further work on the palace. Indra himself decided to leave his life of luxury and relinquish his position as king of the gods to become a hermit and seek wisdom.

Horrified, Indra's wife Shachi asked Brihaspati, the priestly adviser to the gods, to persuade her husband to change his mind. Brihaspati taught Indra to see the virtue of balancing both the spiritual life and the worldly life. Thus, at the end of the story, Indra learned how to pursue wisdom while still fulfilling his kingly duties.

This parable tells us a lot about *manas*. *Manas* has a tendency to get out of control; once something starts building up it goes on and on without limit. *Manas* needs the controlling influence of higher powers – Vishnu and Shiva. This control comes about through gentle instruction leading to humility and knowledge, rather than through forceful restraint. But then *manas* can swing to the other extreme, and cut itself off from its proper function by withdrawing into shame and guilt. Again the intervention of love (Shachi, Indra's wife) and reason (Brihaspati, priest to the gods) restores the balance.

Practices 12 and 13 (see pages 100 and 101) are a couple of simple practices designed to gently restore the proper functioning of *manas*, which will bring a welcome sense of proportion and discernment to the mind.

Buddhi – intellect

Manas is the outermost part of the mind. We are conscious of it because we can hear it chattering and are subject to its machinations. The next part of the inner organ of the mind, *buddhi* or the intellect, is less obvious. The word *buddhi* is defined as 'the power of forming and retaining conceptions and general notions; intelligence, reason, intellect, mind, discernment, judgment; perception, comprehension, apprehension, understanding.'[33] It comes from the root form *budh* meaning to wake up, to observe, to perceive and understand.[34]

Buddhi has the power to discriminate, evaluate and also has the power of creativity. It sifts the information delivered by *manas* and gives it a value: right/wrong; good/bad; useful/useless. As we walk around the streets, go to work, study, chat to our friends or otherwise go about our daily business, we see and hear and otherwise sense innumerable things. Say a smell catches our attention. Perhaps it is a familiar perfume, or perhaps rotting garbage, or diesel exhaust. Immediately the intellect decides on the value or desirability of these sense impressions. Previously we spoke of seeing poor old Jim and burying our head in the newspaper hoping he would pass us by. In these instances a value has been placed on the sense impression. **Practice 14** (see page 101) can give you a sense of the power of *buddhi*.

---

[33] M Monier-Williams, op. cit., p. 733.

[34] ibid.

Discrimination

When *manas* presents its perceptions *buddhi* discriminates by assigning a value and giving meaning to the perception. This discernment and the giving of meaning is a mighty power. If *buddhi* is operating in a clear, strong and focused way then it continuously sifts truth from ignorance, the useful from the useless, and the good from the bad. This is done at every level: food, music, conversation and ideas.

But *buddhi* is dependent on the quality of information coming to it. If *manas* is wandering about, disconnected from reality, then it serves up a diet of past impressions and *buddhi* is then stuck in a habitual loop. These old impressions are only there because some form of decision was made in the past to keep them and store them in memory. We stew over past wrongs for the thousandth time, and revisit our petty triumphs. Or we anticipate future events with craven fear or pathetic hope; and these so-called future events are just another form of dream; they are false predictions born of a mind asleep, based on the partially preserved impressions of a faultily perceived past.

As a test consider how much of the terrifying doom-laden talk of public figures is based on such a bogus view of the future. Economists, politicians, environmentalists (actually just about everyone) pepper their conversations and press releases with actual or implied predictions about the future. How do they know? If you have the time or energy you can check their success rate by rereading past predictions and seeing if any have ever come true. And because virtually none have, it can free you from the fears generated by this sort of doom mongering. Nearly everything that does happen comes as a surprise, pleasant or unpleasant, even to the most respected pundits. The wonder is that no one seems to notice. (Actually it is no wonder, because the ego lives on fear and doubt it easily latches on to news of economic collapse, environmental disaster or rising crime rates to keep us under its magic spell.)

The efforts of politicians, journalists and scientists to appear wiser than they are needn't detain us. The really useful question here is how much of our own inner and outer talk is about the future and how accurate is it? This dream future is the product of recycled ideas and impressions from the past. The solution is to connect *manas* with reality in the present. Failing to do so is referred to in a rather blunt passage in the Bible which tells us of false preachers of whose words Peter says, 'the dog is turned to his own vomit again; and the sow that was washed to her wallowing in the mire.'[35] If we turn again and again to regurgitated sensory memories we tell ourselves over and over again things which are no longer true, and probably never were. We need to strengthen *buddhi*. And this is done in two ways: first by connecting with reality; and secondly, by re-educating it with basic trustworthy principles.

True Principles

Principles are simple statements of obvious, reasonable truth: love your neighbour as yourself; do unto others as you would have them do unto you; this above all to thine own self be true; thou shalt not bear false witness against thy neighbour; the unexamined life is not worth living; live honestly, harm no one and render to every man his due; there should be no compulsion in religion. The preceding list is a fairly random sample with three taken from the Bible, one from Shakespeare, Socrates and Justinian's Institutes; the last from the Koran. The effectiveness of these principles can be tested. **See Practice 15, page 101.**

Buddhi is strengthened with accurate input from *manas*, and with basic statements of spiritual truth. And *buddhi* working effectively is probably the most powerful friend you can have in finding liberation. Another help in getting *buddhi* fit and ready is to pose to the mind questions that you really want the answer to. **See Practice 16, page 102.**

Creative Intelligence

There is another aspect of a clear *buddhi*. It is creative. One easy way of demonstrating this is through the mechanism of resolution. This form of determined decision-making is a very powerful creative tool. When we firmly decide that something will happen, or cease to happen, then it almost seems that the universe rearranges itself to conform. I was standing in front of a whole school assembly which was characteristically noisy and ill-disciplined, which made it difficult to get though the simple business of announcements and also some message for the week. Efforts to get over a hundred young children to sit quietly and still for a few minutes were essentially fruitless and frustrating. One day I felt a shift inside myself. A decision was made that assembly would be quiet and civilised without the staff having to be overly authoritarian. I informed the children and staff of

---

[35] II Peter 2:22.

this decision clearly and resolutely and from then on, assemblies changed for the better. Up until that decision was made nothing really changed – with a few promises and threats the children could be brought to order but it didn't really stick. Since then there are, of course, assemblies which are less settled – but there is a baseline of focused behaviour which it is easy to return to.

People who have successfully given up smoking, or gone on a diet or changed some behaviour in themselves have experienced this creative aspect of *buddhi*. But there is also the aspect of the effect on others. Resolving to see others in a more positive light or ceasing to harbour negativity can change *their* behaviour. Sometimes we simply decide not to put up with another's criticisms or judgments or aggression and we find, surprisingly, that it stops. **See Practice 17, page 102.**

The word *buddhi* is in the feminine form and intelligence is one of the forms of *shakti* or the divine feminine nature, the great mother goddess. In one aspect *buddhi* is personified as the wife of Ganesha, the elephant headed god. Ganesha is a very popular deity in India and there are many affectionate stories told of him, usually showing him to be clever and insightful as befits one who has discrimination, discernment and creativity as his consort.

GANESHA

Ganesha was the son of Lord Shiva and Parwati and he and his brother Kartikeya disputed who was the elder. Shiva proposed a competition: whoever girdled the universe first would be deemed the elder brother. Kartikeya set off swiftly; but Ganesha walked respectfully around his parents saying Shiva and Parwati embodied the whole universe. Ganesha was declared the victor. In another version of the story Ganesha drew the symbol Om, the primordial Word, in the sand and walked around it. The story shows how Ganesha, the husband of Buddhi, ignores peripheral matters and goes to the essence.

Chitta – The Heart

Chitta is the great storehouse of impressions and as such is the seat of our innate nature. While *manas* interprets incoming sensory impressions and passes them to *buddhi* for evaluation, it also draws out from *chitta* an appropriate response to these evaluated impressions. *Chitta* performs several functions, it cognises these impressions, recognises the familiar ones and it stores them away in memory. It is from memory that a response to incoming impressions is drawn out. So Aunt Mabel is seen, the sight of her is handed to *buddhi* which gives a value and a significance to it, *chitta* then cognises it, recognises Aunt Mabel and *manas* draws out of the nearly limitless storehouse of past impressions a response – warmth and love; fear and aversion; greed for her fortune – whatever.

Chitta is like a great warehouse containing who knows what memories, facts, figures, aversions, likes, dislikes, fears, triumphs and so on. These individual bits of information are stored as dimensionless points of knowledge and they have feelings attached to them. And 99.999% of them are unmanifest. They are invisible to our conscious mind, resting inert in the unconscious waiting for the moment when an appropriate stimulus will summon them forth.

Try an experiment: think of the capital of any Asian country … I assume that you weren't thinking of Tokyo, New Delhi or Jerusalem before reading the last sentence. But when asked, the knowledge turned up and was observable in the mind. Where did it come from? What called it out? Assuming it is no longer there, where has it gone? How is it stored in between Geography exams? How can we make the pathway to these stored impressions easy and efficient? All of these questions involve an understanding of *chitta* and the impressions stored there.

Reincarnation

Implicit in much of what I have said so far in this book is the accumulation of karma over long periods of time. Inherent in this is the idea that we accumulate these impressions and claims on experience over many lifetimes. The doctrine of recurrence or reincarnation is the belief that while our physical bodies have a limited life span, our being or soul or individual self – known in Sanskrit as the *jiva* – survives the death of the body, and takes up another physical body in order to continue to live out its karma. This wheel of existence – *samsara* – comes to an end when we gain the ineffable wisdom that we are in fact universal consciousness only, unbound by any physical or subtle body, at which moment we go free of the endless treadmill of limited existence and merge in limitless bliss.

There are two principle alternative views. The Western secular idea that all our existence is essentially physical, that our feelings and beliefs, our theories, thoughts and dreams, our doctrines and cherished fantasies are all the result of bio-electrical and glandular interaction; that mind is brain-based and feelings are the result of glandular secretions. On this view religious and spiritual experience can be explained away as wish-fulfilling internal physical phenomena. And that when brain function ceases we cease to exist in any way, shape or form.

Another view – mainly held by Christians and Muslims – is that we live a single physical life in a universe governed by the commandments of a beneficent, just deity who has laid down immutable laws for living. If we discover and conform to these laws then, when we die we will attain a metaphysical realm of unending bliss – heaven; and if we fail to do so we will be condemned to a place of unending suffering – hell. Some wiggle room is allowed with doctrines such as Limbo and Purgatory, but according to this view you only get one crack at it. How infant death, the suffering of innocents and the occasional triumph of evil is explained raises, for me, more questions than it answers.

It should be fairly clear that each of the above hypotheses is essentially unprovable and faith-based. I will simply say that the doctrine of reincarnation appeals to me, seems the most reasonable, accords with the little personal experience I have of any of these ideas, and has the backing of many saints and sages throughout the millennia of recorded history.

I have also found it immensely practical in teaching children, as it leads to a depth of mutual respect, gives the teacher perspective on the nature and character of the individual child, and is a wonderful corrective to any feelings of condescension due to chronological age.

Happily all of us who adhere to one view or another will find out in the fullness of time whether we were right. The following section explains in more technical detail how reincarnation is supposed to work.

Sanskaras

Impressions, known as *sanskaras,* are created by our emotional response to events. These emotional responses come in three forms. We can like and desire and find pleasure in the event; we can dislike, repel and be averse to the event; or we can ignore, dismiss and be, as it were, asleep to the event. The memory of the event is then stored away for future reference with the emotional marker of like, dislike or indifference. This last one, indifference, should not be confused with the detachment of the wise. It is like turning your back on something hoping it goes away, or like putting your fingers in your ears and singing when you don't want to hear. It is being sleepily oblivious. This is not the attentive, compassionate, fully responsive but uninvolved detachment of the sage.

Sanskaras are divided into three categories: first, *sanchit,* which is the huge unmanifest accumulated store held in *chitta;* secondly *prarabdha,* the small portion of *sanchit* which manifests itself moment by moment in the present in your life; and thirdly *kriyamana* is the *sanskara* created by your response – desire, aversion, indifference – moment by moment to the events of your life. This *kriyamana* is in turn stored as *sanchit* awaiting a stimulus to bring it to the fore. So *sanchit* is your stored past; *prarabdha* is the *sanskara* manifesting in the present; and *kriyamana* is your future.

Being in the Present

On the path to freedom the way out of this rather complex and multi-layered system is to be present, still and responsive to whatever is before you – avoiding the distractions of desire, aversion and indifference. With a clear, uncluttered response to events all the knowledge you need to deal with any situation will be available to you and a perfect response will arise and completely satisfy the needs of the situation. No *kriyamana* is produced and the stored *sanchit* is in some measure dissolved, making us freer and lighter.

But this method of dissolving *sanskaras* will never result in ultimate freedom, because there is simply too much accumulation. If it took millennia to collect, it will take a comparable time to discard, assuming we never accumulate any more. And we spend a lot of our time building up more *sanskaras* simply because we are not totally awake and connected every second of the day. The real power of this practice of responding in the moment is that it brings with it the dawning realisation that, ultimately, we are not our *sanskaras.* We therefore have nothing to dissolve. This is the real knowledge. By habitually giving full attention and, with it, knowledge, intelligence and open-hearted emotion, we learn that the events which manifest in our lives are part of a passing play which we can enjoy and applaud without having to get into costume, get up on stage and start messing up our own and everyone else's lines. **See Practice 18, page 102.**

Our Individual Nature

Chitta is the repository of all those past experiences which we liked, disliked or tried to ignore. It stores these experiences as seedlike points of pure knowledge conjoined with desire or aversion or indifference. It shows itself in the continuous stream of cognition, recognition and memories which rise to meet events. One other interesting aspect of this system is that *sanchit,* taken as a whole, gives us our individual character.

As we repeatedly desire certain things that please us, and reject and flee from things that displease us, and ignore other things that fail to register on our radar, we slowly but surely build up tendencies and inclinations which give us an individual, essentially artificial nature. And we become the sort of person who loves sport, hates reading, won't eat green vegetables and lives in the inner city. Or we like small furry creatures, walks in the sunset and living in the country. And lose our temper when our ideas are challenged; or we see the other chap's point of view; or value strength, or honesty, or kindness. And so on, and so on, and so on, and so on.

Our physical bodies, according to this doctrine, also conform to our nature and to that part of it which, as *prarabdha,* is ready to manifest this lifetime. What body has our accumulated past chosen for us? Which one suits our needs this time? Will we have a human form or not? Our choices are being made right now, moment by moment. How? Our desires pick out the things we like, our aversions reject the things we don't like; and our indifference blinds us to everything else; reinforcing and deepening our nature.

And this happens when we are in waking sleep, when we drive along in a dream while the world passes us by, when we have the same conversation we have had a thousand times before. Our mind – *manas* – weaves these dreams, and these dreams are ephemeral and divorced from reality. By allowing the idle mind to return again and again to the same old familiar subjects and images and objects we are laying down our choices for the future. And much of it is not a pretty sight. Yes, we dream of holidays and good times; but often our dreams are nightmares of anger and resentment and self-criticism and regret. For true freedom and happiness we need to stop both the nightmares and the dreams. We are asleep during both and therefore only have minimal control over either. When we wake up we don't want either, because both dreams and nightmares are binding, and what we want is freedom.

Shiva

In Vedic lore *chitta* is personified as Shiva, also known as Mahesha or the Great God as he stands for Time, Austerity and the ultimate destruction of all ignorance. It would require another book to go into the intricacies and paradoxes of Shiva – the great creative force who also destroys everything; the paradigm of austere chastity and continence whose symbol is the phallus; the benign father of the universe whose host of followers includes the demons. As the personification of *chitta* he holds all the creative potential of the universe.

There are countless stories of Shiva – how he caught the Goddess Ganga in his hair when she descended to earth; how he manifested his third eye – symbol of spiritual insight – when his wife Parvati playfully covered his eyes from behind; and how he lay down in the path of Kali to prevent her from destroying everything.

Perhaps the most recognisable icon of Shiva is the Nataraja – the Lord of the Dance – which shows Shiva dancing out the universal measures of creation. He stands on the dwarf Apasmara – forgetfulness; he has four arms symbolising the four cardinal points of the compass; he holds flame and the Dumru or hourglass-shaped drum representing the union of male and female; and one hand is held in a gesture which banishes fear; he dances within a circle of fire symbolising the wheel of birth and death; and the whole statue stands on a lotus which stands for the boundless creativity of the universe.

Ahankara – The Ego

In the last chapter we dealt with the ego (see page 69). As we discussed, it is the false conjoining of pure being, with a limited aspect of the universe like the body, thoughts, activities and feelings, and it gives us our feeling of selfhood. It is the ruling aspect of the *antahkarana* – the inner organ of mind. It is the chief blockage to real freedom. We become fearful and defensive when this false self is under threat, because we think *we* are under threat. With experience of the true unchanging Self beyond ego, this fear disappears. But until then ego is like a usurper who has stolen the throne of the rightful ruler.

There are thousands of stories of such a dastardly usurper who takes the kingdom from the legitimate king. Shakespeare often used this theme. In *Hamlet* the old king is foully slain while sleeping in his orchard by his brother Claudius, who takes the throne and the queen. Young Hamlet is called upon to slay the usurper and right the wrong. The usurper in *The Tempest, Richard III* and *As You Like It* is a brother, in *Richard II* a cousin, in *Macbeth* a trusted chieftain. These are allegories of the usurpation of the true Self by the ego. Shakespeare, in all these plays, tells us the way to re-establish the rightful order. And in *Twelfth Night* he reveals a more subtle message for us when Olivia says: 'If I do not usurp myself, I am.'

Summary: The Steps So Far

Tanumanasa is the third step on the way to full freedom and happiness. It is the level at which the mind begins to be purified of its accumulations gathered over lifetimes. These accumulations form our nature and habits and weave a spell of ignorance. Under this spell we take the illusory to be real, the trivial to be important and the limited to be eternal. At step one – good impulse – we met a source of wisdom, listened to his or her teachings and took some steps under his or her guidance. At step two, we engaged in some searching enquiry into wisdom and into our own make-up; and we made further efforts to oppose and surrender the habitual parts of our nature. We now, at step three, begin to experience a thinning or attenuation of the mind and its grip on us. We are now ready to take the fourth step on the way to freedom and happiness.

PRACTICE 12 ➤ ➤ ➤ ➤ ➤ ➤ ➤ ➤ ➤

Return with increased enthusiasm to the simple exercise of sitting in a chair connecting with the senses one at a time *(Practice 8, page 74)*. Start with touch – this connects you to your body which is always present; then sight, taste and smell. Finally allow yourself gently to connect with sounds without rushing after and naming and thinking about sounds. Hear 'sound' not 'sounds'. Rest in the awareness.

PRACTICE 13 ➤ ➤ ➤ ➤ ➤ ➤ ➤ ➤ ➤

Follow up the previous practice by stopping as frequently as possible throughout the day just for a few moments before, during and after any activity and connect with any one of the senses. Then continue with the task with increased attention using the most appropriate sense.

PRACTICE 14 ➤ ➤ ➤ ➤ ➤ ➤ ➤ ➤ ➤

Sit quietly and look at some familiar object – perhaps a photograph of a loved one. Try to see the image as merely a collection of lines and surfaces and colours completely divorced from any significance for you on any level. Just let the eyes rest without any other mental activity.

Now allow the mind to 'see' the photo as someone you love and cherish. Observe the feelings, images, anticipations, doubts, hopes and so on which come with this different looking. Now try to return to looking at mere colour and shape and release any feelings of identification and familiarity with the object.

Repeat this process a few times until you feel you are seeing the object, as it were, realistically and objectively without too much overlay of habitual feelings.

PRACTICE 15 ➤ ➤ ➤ ➤ ➤ ➤ ➤ ➤ ➤

Do a little study of some writers and thinkers and artists whose work towards liberation is time-tested. There are the philosophical authors: Plato, Spinoza, Shankara, Confucius, Lao Tse; the scriptural sources: Bible, Gita, Upanishads, Koran, Dhammapada; great poets such as Shakespeare; devotional texts: Mother Teresa, St Teresa of Avila, books of prayers or hymns from any tradition; contemporary writers: Eckhardt Tolle, Lester Levenson, Byron Katie, Brandon Bays.

Find an author or tradition which 'speaks' to you, and then hit on a few phrases or sayings or pieces of advice and if possible memorise them, or just remember the gist, and return to them through the day.

Make use of them by putting them into practice. For example: 'Do unto others …' Try giving everyone what you would want for yourself: courtesy and patience on the roads, a sympathetic hearing, a conscientious day at work, a little space, some of your time, and so on.

PRACTICE 16 ➤ ➤ ➤ ➤ ➤ ➤ ➤ ➤

Sit quietly and still and allow a question to formulate in your mind, such as 'Who am I?' or 'How can I find real freedom?' or 'How can I deal with the situation at work or at home so that no one is harmed?'

Hear the question clearly in mind then send it off as if a butterfly resting on the palm of your hand had gently taken flight. Continue to sit quietly and listen inwardly. Let go of any expectations of any particular answer – or indeed any answer at all.

After a few moments re-sound the question and let it go again. If no clear answer pops in then let the question go a third time, and wait. Then go about your usual activities but be open for the answer.

I often find the answer comes over the next few days or weeks; from my reading or conversations with others or even a snatch of conversation.

PRACTICE 17 ➤ ➤ ➤ ➤ ➤ ➤ ➤ ➤

Try the following:
- Make a firm inner decision that you will give up some form of activity which is troublesome to yourself or others: smoking, over-eating, criticism or other hurtful speech, swearing, some other form of laziness or compulsive behaviour
- Consider someone or something which gives rise to negative feelings (Monday morning, your boss, spouse or colleagues) and resolve to have positive thoughts and feelings
- Think of a situation where you are subject to some form of criticism or negativity and resolve that it will stop.

Be generous with yourself and accept that sometimes these resolutions don't bear immediate fruit. It is worth working with this practice and to keep making efforts. Sometimes action is called for as well. If the boss is unreasonable you may find your inner decision leads to a frank and effective discussion; or a change of careers. Remember it is *buddhi* which decides and it is powerfully creative.

PRACTICE 18 ➤ ➤ ➤ ➤ ➤ ➤ ➤ ➤

Resolve to give full and undivided attention to some task at least three times a day. Pick something fairly ordinary without inherent distraction: walking to the bus stop – feel every footstep; eating breakfast – taste every mouthful; showering – hear sounds, feel sensations. Gently surrender any likes, dislikes, dreams, inner chat and so on.

Make sure this doesn't become a strenuous military operation. Keep it simple, gentle and hopefully, enjoyable.

Chapter **Four**

Step Four:
A State of Clarity

CASE STUDY

A middle-aged woman whose children have started their own families has been meditating and studying Eastern and Western masters for some time. She has been through several stages of inner growth and now finds herself in a serene and peaceful place in herself. Throughout her life she had been plagued by self-doubt and a paralysing fear of confrontation. She would do almost anything to smooth over differences of opinion as her greatest horror had been to be caught in an acrimonious dispute. She would allow others to get the better of her just for a quiet life.

But lately, as she has found her meditation going deeper, and as she has found happiness in surrendering her hold even on her peace and joy, she has found herself more steady and courageous. She has had to speak clearly and confrontingly to tradesmen and sometimes, to members of her family if she felt some injustice was being done. She has been delighted to discover that she has felt free and happy during these conversations and afterwards is untroubled by doubts and second-guessing herself. And she also discovered that, more often than not, the situation resolved itself harmoniously.

Sattvapati

The fourth step on the way to freedom is called *sattvapati*. It represents something of a breakthrough and a staging post. There is stability here which is lacking in the previous stages. At the previous stage of *tanumanasa* there is still the possibility, if we are not vigilant (and sometimes even if we are), that we will succumb to our lower urges. At the level of *sattvapati* the appeal of beguiling habit has largely gone.

An analogy: a chef prepares your favourite meal. She uses the finest ingredients and presents it beautifully; but during the preparation, in plain sight, she mixes in a colourless, tasteless but virulent poison. Tempted? Regardless of how delicious the food looks and smells, few of us would be persuaded to eat it. There would be no effort to hold ourselves back; eating would simply not be an option because 'food which is mixed with poison is itself called poison.'[36]

At the level of *sattvapati*, regardless of egoic payoff we treat our impulses to greed, lust or anger, to which we might previously have given way, like the poison they are. At *sattvapati* it is obvious to us that those inner drives are destructive of peace and happiness. Such impulses still rise in our minds and hearts but they are discriminated without much need for external guidance, encouragement or help, as there is no answering inclination to indulge them. This maturity and access to reason makes *sattvapati* a stable platform below which it is difficult to fall.

An analysis of the meaning of *sattvapati* leads us to consider the Vedic concept of the *gunas*. This basic division of conscious energy into three complementary qualities gives us a very useful framework for our perceptions of the universe and our own internal make-up.

The Three *Gunas*

In the Vedic system there are three conditions or qualities of consciousness called *gunas*. They are *tamas, rajas* and *sattva*. In general *tamas* is inert and unmoving; *rajas* is active and dynamic; and *sattva* is still and serene. Each of the *gunas* has a positive and a negative aspect:

---

[36] AM Sastry, *The Bhagavad Gita,* Samata Books, Madras, 1981, p. 209.

TABLE 3: The *gunas* – qualities of consciousness

	Positive	Negative
Sattva	Serene, peaceful, attentive; consciousness flows uninterruptedly. Words like 'satisfaction' are from the same root as sattva.	Disconnected, dreamy idealism – 'It's all God so why bother'; seeking to prolong spiritual experiences beyond their measure; believing yourself to be further on the path than you are; a false serenity leading to hot anger (rajas) when challenged or pushed to the limits of one's 'comfort zone'.
Rajas	Purposeful, vigorous, lively action and movement. Words like 'regal' and 'royal' come from rajas.	Unbridled frenetic activity, destructive excitement and passion, fanaticism, anger and rage; a state of mental confusion as to right and wrong.
Tamas	Measured, steady; observance of rules and laws, discipline, knowing when to start and when to stop.	Sloth, indolence, sleep, unreasonable fixations, obsessiveness, believing right to be wrong and vice versa; deathlike.

The ever–changing *gunas*

All three *gunas* are present all the time in everything and the balance between them is ever-shifting and changing. While one predominates the other two are ready to take over. One Vedic version of how creation began is that, through desire, the equilibrium of the *gunas* was disturbed. The whole creation consisting of these three elements in differing measures is the result. In Vedic lore Brahma, the Creator, is the embodiment of *rajas*; Vishnu, the Preserver, is the embodiment of *sattva*; and Shiva, the Destroyer, is the embodiment of divine *tamas* in the form of time, law and the natural end of all cosmic cycles.

Our own experience shows us something of the play of the *gunas*, which can be seen in the shifting quality of consciousness throughout the day: where heavy times give way to active, even frenetic, times; and other periods of the day – sunrise, sunset, twilight – have a natural stillness and calm. The year also reflects this, with certain seasons having a tendency to inertia and others having a lively vitality, and still others having a sense of peace and serenity. Foods, music, animals, places, even buildings have their characteristic *guna* balance.

Pilgrimage sites

Places where people have worshipped, sacrificed and done good works have a feel of *sattva*. This makes these places uplifting and they attract devotion and reverence which creates more *sattva*. Pilgrimage sites across the world attract millions of devotees for this very reason, adding further to the power of the site. The Kumbha Mela, a massive gathering of millions of devotees at the confluence of the Ganges and Jumna Rivers, held every twelve years, is one such phenomenon. Well-known pilgrimage sites like Canterbury, Santiago de Compostella, Rome, Mecca and Jerusalem also have a compelling atmosphere that mere stones and architecture cannot explain.

I visited the Al Aqsa Mosque in Jerusalem some years ago and on entering I experienced a state of complete stillness, peace and universality without any personal effort. I had a similar experience when I first saw Leonardo's cartoon of *The Virgin and Child with St Anne and John the Baptist* in the National Gallery in London.

A few years ago the school where I work needed to relocate. We bought our new premises from a church group which trained missionaries to work among the unfortunate and the dispossessed. When we took over the property many of us commented on the goodness in the atmosphere. And subsequently, others have been kind enough to comment on the atmosphere now, in a place dedicated to teaching children not only their times tables and grammar, but also about consciousness and how to live a life which is both happy and reasonable and a help to others.

The other *gunas* can also predominate in certain places. Some cities or indeed nations are naturally rajasic. The active quality of New York has been captured in catchy phrases which eulogise its bustle and energy – 'it's a helluva town', 'a city that doesn't sleep', 'so good they named it twice'! While, perhaps, not a patch on New York, Sydney, my home town, has a drive and buzz which make it an exciting place to live and work. There is a sense that anything is possible. On the other hand there is an edge to Sydney, while Melbourne has a calmer air which, for a Sydneysider, gives a welcome break.

More ominously some places can carry the atmosphere of dark deeds. An acquaintance of mine told me how she was travelling around the highlands of Scotland. She was lost and as she was driving through a particular valley she felt an inner cold and fear verging on horror. The feeling passed as she left the valley and only later did she find out she had been at Glencoe, scene of the infamous massacre of the McDonald clan.

People and their *guna* balance

Everyone has a mixture of all three *gunas* – we all need a measure of activity, sleep and serenity. Nevertheless, we also have a tendency for one to outweigh the others. Some people are therefore said to be *tamasic,* some *rajasic* and others *sattvic.* When operating positively each of these three types of people function well: *tamasic* people are disciplined, measured and follow the rules. They may also be a bit stodgy, but at their best, they know when to get going on an activity and when to stop; rajasic people are active, lively, vital and energetic; sattvic people are peaceful, centred and integrated.

As we saw in Table 3 these *guna* balances in people also have negative aspects: inertia and stubbornness and a tendency to cling to false opinions *(tamas)*; frenetic activity, doubt and an edgy, brittle touchiness *(rajas)*; a dreamy, unrealistic, don't bother me, 'space-cadet' attitude *(sattwa)*.

Sometimes there can be a propitious or unpropitious mix. *Rajas* and *tamas* together can lead to destructive fanaticism or a sort of fixed evil: When I was a solicitor I encountered a well-known Sydney criminal at the Supreme Court. He had a history of violence and was walking in with his legal team. He had the air of a feral animal with a coldness in his eyes which was truly frightening. He had, in the terms we are speaking of, an extreme measure of negative *tamas* and *rajas.* While it is not my policy to wish others harm, a few years later this man met an untimely end at the hands of his, ahem, business rivals, and I'm afraid to say, when I heard the news I felt the world was a better place.

The cultivation of *sattva*

The basic rule here is that when *sattva* is predominant then the other two *gunas* work healthily. When either *rajas* or *tamas* are in the ascendant, and when we swing from one to the other, things can go awry. Frenetic excitement, passion and partying lead to a collapse into inertia. Indecision and lethargy lead to precipitous, disastrous action – either jumping too early, or leaving it too late.

We all encounter *tamas* and *rajas* in the natural course of daily events – in sleep, rest and inertia; and in activity, work and movement. We also meet them as stodgy confusion, doubt, activity, chatter and streaming images in mind. *Sattva* on the other hand is rarer and needs to be cultivated consciously. While we may encounter occasional moments of tranquillity and peace, most of us need to consciously develop the self-contained inner tranquillity of *sattva*.

How do we do this? The practices and disciplines recommended by the wise cultivate *sattva*. Some of these have been included in this book. An essential feature of any method of enlightenment is that it encourages us to accumulate *sattva* – that quality of consciousness which is still and tranquil, attentive, ready to respond but remains undisturbed.

The good news is that *sattva* is always available and you don't need to do much to get some. Taking a few moments each day to connect with the present moment; listening attentively to yourself and others; reading some uplifting literature – this will accumulate *sattva*. You don't need very much of it to feel a difference in your being. When the prodigal son arose and started on his homeward journey 'he was yet a great way off, [when] his father saw him, and had compassion, and ran, and fell on his neck, and kissed him.'[37] Our halting efforts get a mighty pay off; just a few minutes a day of genuine effort to wake up and be present result, in a very short time, in a palpable change in our being.

Having practised a few of the exercises in this book you will surely have felt a rise in consciousness, a greater focus and perhaps a growing sense of an inner Self beyond the harum-scarum ups and downs of the ego. All this indicates an accumulation of *sattva*.

---

[37] Luke 15:20.

Features of *sattvapati*

Sattvapati means entering into a state or condition of *sattva* where finer energy is available allowing us to be steady, focused and conscious. There is light in the mind which highlights shortcomings, and gives us the clarity and strength to discard them. The need for continuous guidance from a teacher or system is therefore reduced. The efficient use of energy leads to a diminution of sentimentality, and there is a natural determination to live a good, truthful life.

One other notable feature of *sattvapati* is a reduction of fear. Fear has both a *rajasic* aspect which sets the mind and heart racing and a *tamasic* aspect which freezes us and renders us indecisive and incapable of effective action. At *sattvapati* our confidence grows and our fears shrink. We feel strong so the danger of succumbing to temptation is greatly reduced. We feel inwardly powerful and have integrity and courage and look forward now to the next steps on our journey.

Integrity

Integrity, basic honesty and trustworthiness in our dealings with others, comes about because all our faculties of intellect and feeling line up and do their jobs properly – they are integrated. The opposite state – disintegration (sometimes literally) – is when we try to think with our feelings, or allow our thoughts to race while our bodies are paralysed. **See Practice 19, page 121.**

Genesis: The Fourth Day – Lights in the firmament

And God said, let there be lights in the firmament of the heaven to divide the day from the night; and let them be for signs, and for seasons, and for days, and for years; and let them be for lights in the firmament of the heaven to give light upon the earth: and it was so. And God made two great lights; the greater light to rule the day, and the lesser light to rule the night: he made the stars also.[38]

---

[38] Genesis 1:14-16.

This vivid description can help us with our understanding of *sattvapati*. On the fourth day God sets lights in the heavenly firmament. Like the *gunas* these heavenly lights are three in number: the greater light, the lesser light and the stars. And they have three tasks: to divide the day from the night; to establish measures of time (the seasons, the day and the year); and to give light to the earth.

The unnamed sun, moon and stars

One curious fact about day four is that, while God names Heaven, Earth, Day, Night, Seas and so on, He seems rather pointedly to leave the heavenly lights unnamed. Why? One suggestion is that, because these three were central to the pagan religions of the Egyptians, Canaanites and Mesopotamians, the author of Genesis wanted to demote them. He puts them in their place, as it were, by leaving them unnamed, by relegating them to the fourth day and by indicating that they are totally dependent on God for their existence. The author of Genesis thereby makes the point that they are subordinate, essentially mechanical and of a distinctly ungodly nature.

What does this tell us of *sattvapati?* The hint here is that our minds and hearts can experience great illumination as we move towards full realisation, but we shouldn't mistake these momentary flashes of light, which encourage us to continue on our way, for ultimate enlightenment. By indicating their subsidiary nature we are warned not to treat a burst of inspiration and insight as final liberation.

The lights rule the day and the night

Genesis tells us that these lights rule the day and the night. The 'day' represents our good times, when we are focused and disciplined and keen to be awake. The day is the time of mental clarity and illumination, like an inner beacon of light.

But we all experience moments of darkness as well on our spiritual journey, when we feel that our efforts are less fruitful and our enthusiasm flags. Even in darkness we have help – the light that rules the night – which is the guidance, knowledge and insight we receive from our teachers; it is a light which seems to come from outside ourselves.

The great light and the lesser light are single, obvious and unmistakable, and guide those who are looking for a way out of their darkness, misery and ignorance. But for those who have yet to begin the search the stars symbolise the plethora of hints, pointers and clues scattered generously throughout the creation for people whose ears and eyes are on the verge of being attuned to a higher way. They are points of illumination which show us that there is always light in the surrounding darkness.

The aspirant at the level of *sattvapati* always has one of these forms of light available. They are actually moving in the light all the time and have direct experience of its help; and hence he or she isn't tempted by those distractions which wrong-footed them at the earlier levels.

Another meaning for the greater light to rule the day and the lesser light to rule the night is the division of our nature into a manifest and an unmanifest part. The implication is that while we are clear about our manifest nature – our personality, how we interact with others, our strengths and weaknesses – our subconscious unmanifest nature is, by definition, hidden from view. On day four both aspects – conscious and unconscious – come under the light and feel the effects of the healing balm of *sattva*.

The lights measure out the seasons, the day and the year

The lights are 'for signs, and for seasons, and for days, and for years'. These measured time periods give us insight into a key characteristic of *tamas* – the right time to do some things and not to do others. It connects us to the temporal cycles of the universe from the greatest to the least. To know this is a mighty gift. As it says in Ecclesiastes, Chapter 3:

1   *To every thing there is a season, and a time to every purpose under the heaven:*

2   *A time to be born, and a time to die; a time to plant, and a time to pluck up that which is planted;*

3   *A time to kill, and a time to heal; a time to break down, and a time to build up;*

4   *A time to weep, and a time to laugh; a time to mourn, and a time to dance;*

5   *A time to cast away stones, and a time to gather stones together; a time to embrace, and a time to refrain from embracing;*

6   *A time to get, and a time to lose; a time to keep, and a time to cast away;*

7   *A time to rend, and a time to sew; a time to keep silence, and a time to speak;*

8   *A time to love, and a time to hate; a time of war, and a time of peace.*

Just consider verse seven. What would we give simply to know when to keep silence and when to speak? At *sattvapati* we have this knowledge.

The earth is illumined

And this leads to the final task of these heavenly lights: to light the earth. The earth stands for our individual being, and these lights illuminate our nature, our attributes, our strengths and weaknesses so that we can move forward with clear, honest self-examination. As US Supreme Court Justice Louis Brandeis said: 'sunlight is the best disinfectant'. It should be noted that, at *sattvapati*, it appears to us that the illumination is externally sourced. We are deepening our access to inner light but the guidance and inspiration still seem to us to come from a source outside ourselves.

The Effect of *Sattva* on Others

But others are beginning to see this differently. With all this illumination our words, actions and our very being become a source of light and *sattva* for others. In the previous three steps the good company of others helped us avoid pitfalls. Now, at level four, we have become good company for others; because we live in the light we become a beacon for those who come within our sphere. Situations can often transform themselves in our presence. A condition of chaos or aggression might settle down; seemingly intractable problems find solutions which are, as they say, obvious when they are pointed out. The man or woman at level four radiates *sattva* and *sattva* brings *rajas* and *tamas* under control. Actions and words become more measured and lawful and appropriate.

The person at the level of *sattvapati* is often only marginally aware of this effect on others. And when they do observe the effect on others, rather than pride in their own glory, they feel humble and grateful. Those at lower levels of development who feel the effects of the *sattva* radiating from these people can't fully grasp what has happened. In fact it may seem almost miraculous. I saw a deeply troubled little boy who was tantrumming violently and needed physical restraint to protect himself and others, calm down immediately when a wonderful and deeply spiritual friend of mine walked into the room. She didn't seem to 'do' anything – her mere presence did the trick.

While we might not understand precisely a person at a higher level, generally we can say that they *are* at a higher level because of the way we feel in their presence, and the effect of their words, their actions and their uncanny knack of meeting the need exactly. All these give a good indication of their higher stage of development. People at this level are not common. But when you meet someone with a preponderance of *sattva* you generally remember it. I went to see Leon MacLaren when I was appointed headmaster. I had to write down my concerns and questions, because I found in his presence nothing seemed to be a problem, and I tended to forget to ask about issues which reasserted their importance when he was no longer around.

People often speak about the effect of meetings with remarkable men and women. Friends of mine are devotees of Amma, Sri Mata Amritanandamayi Devi, and their descriptions of how they feel in her presence are wonderfully inspiring. These friends radiate *sattva* when speaking of Amma.

Earlier I mentioned a friend who, on seeing Swami Tejomayananda of the Chinmaya Mission, knew immediately that she had found her teacher. I met her some years later at a lecture by the Swami in Sydney. Not having seen each other for some years we chatted amiably. As we spoke a queue of Indian people bowed to her and offered her homage. She gave each one a radiant smile as she kept up the conversation with me. Their worship and her ego-free acceptance was beautiful and, standing next to her I felt bathed in love and bliss. It was profoundly moving and it was also a great lesson in true humility. She stood out like a beacon and was being adored and venerated, without the slightest taint of ego. She was completely open and natural, and everyone, including me, received her gift of love and happiness.

These are examples of people with *sattva* in their being. They seem lit from within and have a healing effect on others. People like this occupy or have passed through the fourth level or middle of the seven levels of humanity.

The Seven Levels of Humanity

In this scheme humanity is organised into two main parts – an inner circle consisting of levels five, six and seven who teach; and an outer circle – levels one, two and three – who learn (all going well).

The outer circle

Those in the outer circle of humanity are engaged in the normal activities of life: getting and spending, avoiding pain and pursuing pleasure, and doing the best they can for themselves and their families and their communities. When they die, if they have done well, they are eulogised as decent family men or women who raised their children and were pillars of the community. After a few years the memory fades and, for most of us, it is as if we had never been. In this outer circle even the memory of the mighty fades. As Shelley says of one such arrogant Pharoah:

> *And on the pedestal these words appear:*
> *'My name is Ozymandias, king of kings:*
> *Look on my works, ye Mighty, and despair!'*
> *Nothing beside remains. Round the decay*
> *Of that colossal wreck, boundless and bare*
> *The lone and level sands stretch far away.*[39]

In the Katha Upanishad Death offers Nachiketas riches, long life and other delights of life in the outer circle. Nachiketas, wanting access to the inner circle, says dismissively (and rather bravely), compared with eternity 'the longest life is short'.[40]

But the survival of humanity is utterly dependant on this vast sea of men and women who dwell in the outer circle attending to their daily duties and responsibilities; a few attaining fame and riches, most faithfully leading the ordinary lives of decent householders: getting up each morning, getting the kids off to school, and going to work to do the best by their clients and customers and employers and employees. It is not necessarily

---

[39] Percy Bysshe Shelley, 'Ozymandias'.
[40] *Ten Principal Upanishads,* op. cit., p. 28.

glorious work memorialised in story or song or statue, but, almost literally, it makes the world go round. Such a life has its ups and downs; and some faithfully stick as best they can to their duty, while others, through low cunning or stupidity, fail to do so, leaving others to work harder to clean up the mess. Such is the outer circle of humanity.

Let not Ambition mock their useful toil,
Their homely joys, and destiny obscure;
Nor Grandeur hear with a disdainful smile
The short and simple annals of the Poor,

The boast of heraldry, the pomp of power,
And all that beauty, all that wealth e'er gave,
Awaits alike th' inevitable hour:-
The paths of glory lead but to the grave.[41]

The outer circle – levels one, two and three

Within this outer circle there is a threefold hierarchy: the first level consists of people ruled by appetite; the second, those ruled by faith; and the third, those ruled by intellect. An individual can move up or down the scale, but without guidance and conscious effort we tend to default to one of the three levels. The key feature of each of these levels, and of the outer circle as a whole, is that they are all more or less mechanical. In other words the denizens of these lower three levels are reactive and are mostly ruled by stimulus and response; internal, habitual reactions meeting the unceasing flow of external events.

Level one, the lowest level, consists of those ruled by appetite. They act on the basis of their own pleasure and pain – yearning for the one, and fleeing from the other. There is little room in their field of consideration for anyone else – even family and friends may be sacrificed when push comes to shove. But, in ordinary circumstances, those at level one work and live reasonably decent unexceptional lives, restrained from the broader excesses of their appetites by the laws and rules of society. Their

---

[41] Thomas Gray, 'Elegy Written in a Country Church-Yard'.

obedience to these rules is largely through fear of the consequences of wrongdoing – gaol, fines and other penalties. When those entrusted by society with upholding the laws cease to do so through corruption, cowardice or a loss of will, and the enforcement of the laws begins to wane, people at level one are largely off the leash. They seek to satisfy their selfish whims and society as a whole becomes a less cohesive and more dangerous place.

At level two there is a certain opening of the heart. Here faith – sometimes blind faith – rules. This is often, but not necessarily, religious faith. It can be political and ideological faith; and others – members of the family, community or nation or religion – are included in the circle of care and consideration. But we can have faith in all sorts of things and ideas and people, not all of them benign. There can be loyalty to the teachings of a church or mosque or synagogue, or faith in an ideology of social responsibility. Or devotion at this level can become the fanaticism of the football fan or the pop groupie. And it can also descend into faith in a cruel, mass murdering tyrant – Mao Tse Tung, Stalin or Hitler. These charismatic leaders can beguile those at this level in their masses.

The third level is that of intellect. Those at this level, to a certain extent, think for themselves. Life can take on a more reasonable cast. But here faith is questioned and perhaps even scorned; cynicism and a sort of shallow argumentativeness can also take hold, where matters of devotion or feeling are mocked and undermined simply because those who feel them lack the sophisticated vocabulary of these pseudo-intellectuals. Those at level three may be able to weave sophisticated arguments, but they lack the compassion, understanding and humility which are the hallmarks of men and women of true intellect.

For the outer circle to maintain a healthy course over the long term it needs regular guidance and input from men and women of wisdom; and this is where the inner circle comes in.

The inner circle

The inner circle is where men and women of higher consciousness live and work. They have knowledge, devotion, insight and power, and an understanding of the real inner workings of themselves, mankind and the universe. Often hidden, some show themselves at regular intervals in history to guide and instruct the majority of humanity who dwell in the outer circle. These master teachers of mankind appear, when necessary, as prodigies, artists, painters or writers; as prophets, leaders of esoteric or philosophical schools, men and women of insight; as founders of the major religions and as the perfected sages and saints. This inner circle is also divided into three levels: level five, six and seven. These three levels consist of teachers, prophets and the fully enlightened.

The common feature of those who dwell here is that they are awake, and their lives are not ruled by habit or sleep. Their teachings are always available to those who, in Jesus's words, 'have ears to hear'. In many of His parables He refers to those who get the message and those who don't. He taught in parables so those whose ears were open would catch the inner meaning, and those whose ears were not open would listen anyway. Other teachers use poetry (Shakespeare) or music (Mozart) or philosophical discourse (Plato, Socrates, Aristotle) or religious principles (Moses, Mohammed, Buddha). Some teachers remain hidden from the outer circle but send their disciples out to teach; others, through their meditations, send out pulsating conscious energy to any who need it. **See Practice 20, page 122.**

Level four

Men and women at level four have attained the stage of *sattvapati*. This level fills the gap between the mechanical outer circle, and the conscious and aware inner circle and is crucial to mankind's health and development. The people at this level have a hybrid nature. They partake of the duties and responsibilities of the outer world – earning a living, supporting their family, taking part in the community and adhering to the laws and dictates of society. At the same time they are aware that there is something greater than mere mundane existence, and that there are higher laws to be obeyed. The role of those at level four is to seek out and follow the guidance of the wise at the higher levels.

They also have the task of formulating this universal wisdom into a language and system which those at the lower levels can follow. Shakespeare spoke of the difficulty that those in the outer circle have in hearing this divine wisdom: 'such harmony is in immortal souls, but whilst this muddy vesture of decay doth grossly close us in, we cannot hear it.' [42] He also out-lined the pivotal role of those at level four who can hear the higher levels:

> *The poet's eye, in a fine frenzy rolling,*
> *Doth glance from heaven to earth,*
> *From earth to heaven;*
> *And, as imagination bodies forth*
> *The forms of things unknown,*
> *The poet's pen turns them to shapes,*
> *And gives to airy nothing*
> *A local habitation and a name.* [43]

Thus universal love becomes 'love thy neighbour as thyself'; absolute justice becomes 'innocent until proven guilty'; faith may appear as 'There is no God but Allah'; compassion as the care and stewardship of the environment. The laws of divine harmony may be formulated as the principles of a school of architecture, music or poetry. In a Western cultural context the Mona Lisa, Hamlet, Chartres Cathedral or Mozart's *Mass in C Minor* can be seen as reflecting the wisdom of a higher level. But of course, the works of Confucius, the temples of Angkor Wat, the philosophy of Shankara, and the finest music, literature, art and architecture of every people on earth reflect the beauty, harmony and universal wisdom of the higher levels.

Level four comes and goes

There are always people at the levels other than level four, but level four is only occupied when the outer circle needs a new flow of wisdom from the inner circle. The result is a refreshment of spiritual principles and often an explosion of artistic creativity, of wealth and philosophical and scientific enquiry. When this work has been done level four is again left vacant and the direct flow of consciousness from the inner to the outer circle ceases. But the role of guiding the outer circle is filled by institutions, customs, works of artistic genius and systems of law and justice which were established when this level was occupied.

---

[42] William Shakespeare, *The Merchant of Venice*, act 5, scene 1.

[43] William Shakespeare, *A Midsummer Night's Dream,* act 5, scene 1.

Over time, however, these institutions become a little rusty with age. In the never-ending play of the *gunas*, the *sattva* in the founding laws and principles of these institutions slowly leaches out over time and *tamas* begins to do its work. A school of art which begins as a fresh, vibrant and ground breaking way of presenting the beauty of the creation becomes fixed and hide-bound and sterile. Forms of government based on principles of justice and law become inflexible and begin, in time, to create injustice. As these institutions begin to run out of steam and get tired and worn, the clever intellectuals at level three begin to question the validity of the old order, and to apply their intellect to tearing them down; the faithful at level two become confused and filled with doubt and begin to put their faith in just about anything which catches their attention; and those governed by appetite begin to throw off the restraint of law and simple decency. Then level four needs to be re-occupied.

The wise of the inner circle put out a subtle call which is heard by people of the outer circle who are ready to take a step towards enlightenment. They begin to look for guidance, and often a movement or school of human development, initiated by the wise, arises and trains up willing seekers who begin to occupy the vacancy at level four.

Initially these people may not know this is where they are heading. They just feel a certain lack in their lives, come across a guide or teaching and take up the quest. They are of the outer circle, speak its language and understand its ways, but they begin the work to clear their minds and senses and they start to hear the sound of wisdom – to develop ears that hear. They get a feeling for the natural order of the universe, for its laws and the intelligence behind its operations. And they take this understanding and shape it, in their own way; to translate it into song or speech, architecture or medicine, art or law; and, historically after a generation or so, these new ways begin to catch on and a Renaissance flowers.

When these people at level four, the level of *sattvapati*, have done their job they move on to the higher levels, leaving in place institutions and customs to guide the community for centuries until the next period of inertia calls forth another similar group.

'Tell my story'

One day I was watching a production of Hamlet and, as the bodies were piling up on stage, Horatio was holding the dying Hamlet in his arms and he took the poisoned goblet and announced that he would follow Hamlet in death. But Hamlet stopped him. He asked Horatio to 'report me and my cause aright to the unsatisfied', and he tells him that it is not his time to die: 'Absent thee from felicity awhile, and in this harsh world draw thy breath in pain, to tell my story.' [44] In a moment of clear insight, I knew without a shadow of doubt, that these were the instructions given to Shakespeare by his master, and that Shakespeare faithfully carried out these instructions for decades, penning thirty-seven plays, over 150 sonnets and other sundry poems. These are works which four centuries later continue to entertain, delight and intrigue and which also contain profound esoteric wisdom. In terms I am now using, Shakespeare stayed at level four formulating the wisdom of the inner circle. He knew the secret world of hidden wisdom and he gave it 'a local habitation, and a name'.

Summary

At the first three stages on the journey to freedom and happiness the ever-present help of a guide or teacher is necessary to overcome impulses and temptations laid in our path. Then, at the level of *sattvapati*, there is a welcome relief from the struggle and vulnerability of the previous phases. *Sattva* gives us the power to choose, and the ability and the will to choose correctly. It also makes us a source of help and uplift to others, which brings a certain responsibility to use that gift wisely. We have received that access to *sattva* largely through the help and compassion of those who have gone before us and we in turn would do well to reach out a helping hand to those who are coming after. So those who have attained *sattvapati* naturally take to teaching and propagating the wisdom they have received; in doing so they prepare themselves to continue to the next level of *asangsakti*.

---

[44] William Shakespeare, *Hamlet,* act 5, scene 2.

PRACTICE 19 ➤ ➤ ➤ ➤ ➤ ➤ ➤ ➤ ➤

This exercise is adapted from Plato's *Republic,* Book IX, and is designed to integrate our different centres.

Sit quietly and engage your visual imagination: you will be asked to visualise three images one after the other and then all three at once. This practice is enjoyable and illuminating.

First, imagine a voracious many-headed monster. This monster is hungry but is never satisfied. And the heads are all different – monkey, elephant, dragon, human – and they are constantly changing shape. Establish this vivid image and then store it away.

Next image is a lion – fierce, energetic, passionate and dangerous. Establish this image clearly in your mind and then store that one away as well.

Now imagine a man – reasonable, steady, dependable, intelligent and keep him in mind.

Now imagine that this reasonable man is inside your head; then feel the image of the lion inside your chest under the control and guidance of the reasonable man; now add the many-headed beast in your stomach under the firm but just control of the man and guided by the energy and passion of the lion.

This, according to Plato, is a human being with his or her faculties in their correct relationship to each other. According to him, integrity comes about when passion (the lion) and appetite (the many-headed beast) are ruled by reason (the man). We know all too well what life is like when our unreasonable passions and infatuations rule us; or when our unbridled desires and appetites hold sway. But, at the same time, if we spend all our time reasoning without ever acting or engaging our emotions, we are similarly incapable of living effectively. When one centre tries to do the work of another, it leads to disintegration.

PRACTICE 20 ➤ ➤ ➤ ➤ ➤ ➤ ➤ ➤ ➤

Sit somewhere quiet and relax. Go inside yourself and rest quietly listening to the silence within. Feel the presence of an underlying flow of consciousness permeating your body, mind and heart. Feel it as a flow of knowledge and wisdom available to anyone who wants or needs guidance. Gently open yourself to receiving wisdom or understanding.

Reflect on some dilemma or issue which you want clarified. Who am I? When will I be free? What should I do next? How can I best serve others?

And wait for the limitless wisdom to reveal itself. As with other practices of this type it is best to be light and gentle; and to be patient and repeat the exercise if an answer (or indeed a question) doesn't pop in immediately.

*   *   *   *   *   *   *

Chapter **Five**

Step Five:
Insight and Detachment

CASE STUDY

A man has been following his teacher's guidance for some time and has worked through the earlier levels of effort and practice – working against his negative tendencies. He has reached a level where he feels an inner steadiness and is able to see things clearly and also to be a source of clarity for others. Now he begins to experience a deeper vision of things as woven of consciousness only. He finds a well-spring of warmth and love for everything he sees. This includes his own thoughts and feelings which he watches with detachment and interest. Good and bad, right and wrong cease to have significance for him. Not that he is unaware of others' suffering, but he sees things as essentially like a drama or play with everyone and everything playing a part. It may be a tragedy or a comedy but the most important thing is who the 'actor' really is – pure consciousness – rather than the temporary part they're playing. On first realising this state he sometimes finds it hard to give full credence to the ups and downs of life which others find so significant. But gradually he discovers a way of acting and responding and speaking and a vocabulary where he can connect with others and communicate effectively. Some begin to recognise that he has a light and an ease about him and seek him out for advice and guidance which he is happy to give. And he lightly side-steps the egoic desire to become an object of veneration and reverence to these people.

Asangsakti

We now come to *asangsakti*, the fifth step on the way to freedom and happiness. The word *asangsakti* means 'the power of detachment'. At this stage we see beyond the appearance of things and objects are experienced as consciousness only. Seeing the source of everything as consciousness, we cease to see separation but know everything to be fundamentally related. There is no conflict or disharmony. At the level of *asangsakti* we love the whole world as our family.

MONEY ON THE TABLE

A wise man used to come home from work each payday and he would put his wages on the dining room table. Anyone could take what they needed. His wife complained about this, and he pointed out that she was not excluded from this and could take as much or as little as she needed as well. The whole world was his family.

This way of dealing with our salaries may not seem a practical option for us; nevertheless, even if we have not yet arrived at *asangsakti*, many of us are very conscious of the needs of others. Many give time to voluntary work or money to charities. We are deeply moved by the suffering of people we will never meet. These are glimmers of the universal feeling; they give a foretaste of one feature of *asangsakti* – the refinement of love where differences cease to be important.

The Story So Far

How do we arrive at this loving condition where we experience unifying consciousness? The first three steps, as we have seen, need the guidance, care and knowledge of a teacher. While treading these three steps, and despite occasional experiences of limitless unity, we take the reality of ordinary world with its differentiated forms for granted. We also believe in the reality of ourselves as separate beings, our egos, our personalities, our desires and aversions. The wise tell us that these worldly forms are illusory but at levels one, two and three we give ourselves and our world a significance and reality which they do not in truth possess.

Think back to your teenage years with its infatuations and heartbreaks, the concerns about music, fashions and friendships. How important do they seem now? Things that seemed a matter of life and death now mean nothing. At *asangsakti* the things which previously set your world in a spin are similarly known to be meaningless. Seeing everything as an emanation of unifying consciousness, then separation and conflict cease.

And science confirms this alternative view of reality. At a quantum level the physical world exists mostly as empty space. And these empty physical bodies which we ride around in all day are all ultimately heading for the recycling centre. If we examine our thoughts and feelings they are similarly ephemeral and intangible, and exist as energy only. This body/mind is an illusory shape on a journey towards oblivion, which we cling to with tiger-like ferocity. It doesn't make sense on any level, so most of us do the logical thing: we don't think about it.

Those of us who do ponder these paradoxes, and start to show signs of wanting to be free receive help; and if we follow the advice of those ahead of us on the journey we progress, and feel less burdened by the cares which ordinary life throws up. We discover inner powers which previously were only dimly suspected, and begin to see the world as consciousness only.

Letting Go of Feeling Good

The first three steps can be repeated over and over again: first, a bit of good impulse, some wise advice, a hot tip for liberation; then secondly, some effort and enquiry leading to a struggle with old habits and tendencies; and, finally, the mind purifies, the tendencies loosen their grip and we feel freer. As we saw in Chapter Three, we often relax at level three. After all, the problem has gone away, the world beckons, and the incentive for going free is no longer there because, relatively speaking, we *are* free. But, as Lester Levenson often said, 'release when you're high!' The key to moving beyond level three and moving on to the higher stages is to transcend and detach from the good, positive and pleasant experiences and feelings brought about by the work at the first three levels.

In the *Aparokshanubhuti* a short work by Adi Shankara he tells us that in the practice of *samadhi* – a deeply meditative state – there are many unavoidable obstacles which include the usual suspects such as idleness, sleep and distraction; but he also includes the 'tasting of joy'.[45]

---

[45] Swami Vimuktananda (trans.), *Aparokshanubhuti: Self Realization of Sri Sankaracharya,* Advaita Ashrama, Calcutta, 1989, p. 69 vs 128.

The first blockage to surrendering this 'tasting of joy' is that it simply doesn't occur to us. And secondly, when it is brought to our attention that we should, we don't want to. Why let go of feeling good? The answer is, if we stop working when the pressure of misery is off, we will never be truly free. If we try to hold on to the feeling of wakefulness and freedom which comes from our efforts to be present, this guarantees that we will face the same misery again.

The negative aspect of *sattva* is this tendency to hold on to and prolong experiences of enlightenment. These then become mere memories which replay like any other circling thought – jostling for time and attention with feelings of guilt, doubt, self-loathing, anger, jealousy and so on. And the darker thoughts and feelings are much better at getting our attention. As we keep returning to memories of spiritual highs they may become tinged with regret, a sense of loss or nostalgia where, by comparison, the present seems dull and empty. The following story offers an example.

MANNA FROM HEAVEN

When the Children of Israel were in the Wilderness after their escape from slavery in Egypt they ran out of food and water and complained to Moses that they had been brought out of Egypt only to starve to death. At Moses' request God delivered manna from heaven. This mysterious food covered the ground each morning and everyone was instructed to gather only as much as they needed to feed themselves and their families for one day. They were to consume their portion that day and not try to store it overnight. There was no need to hoard because sufficient manna would appear each day. But guess what? 'Notwithstanding they hearkened not unto Moses, but some of them left of it until the morning, and it bred worms, and stank: and Moses was wroth with them.'[46]

What a surprise.

This story illustrates the need for a little trust, and the perils of squirrelling away experiences of liberation for a rainy day. They turn wormy and putrid – they are transformed into burdensome self-chat and nostalgic memory. Rather than hoarding, let them go and allow a flow of experience.

---

[46] Exodus 16:20.

The Manna story goes on to tell us of those that followed the rule of only taking what was needed:

> ... *he that gathered much had nothing over, and he that gathered little had no lack; they gathered every man according to his eating.*[47]

Moving up the scale

At level three, *tanumanasa,* we have developed the ability to relinquish negative habits. The shift from level three to four comes about largely by continuous practice and by letting go of the good tendencies and feelings and ceasing to identify with them. This creates a flow where, rather than losing these feelings of well-being, peace and detachment, we experience more.

The advice of the wise is to let pleasant and uplifting feelings and tendencies go free. There will be plenty of love left over. A water pipe is not depleted of water when the tap is turned on. Rather it fills again with fresh water ready for the next time someone is thirsty. When a child is born the parents give it all their love, and when a second child comes along they don't have to get back fifty-percent of their love so they can share it out equally. Thus everyone knows from their own experience that love is limitless, except when we try to hold onto this limitless love and keep a portion for ourselves.

I am hammering this point because we cannot progress to *asangsakti* and beyond without releasing our hold on both negative and positive feelings. The key realisation is that we already have limitless love, consciousness and insightful intelligence. We block access to them by hoarding past experiences of love, consciousness and insight which turns them into repetitive thoughts and feelings.

Put simply, we desire what we already have. This was the transgression of Adam and Eve. Eve saw the forbidden fruit of the tree of the knowledge of good and evil, and she had three separate motives for taking and eating it:

> *And when the woman saw that the tree was good for food, that it was pleasant to the eyes, and a tree to be desired to make one wise, she took of the fruit thereof and did eat.*[48]

---

[47] Exodus 16:18.

[48] Genesis 3:6.

The fruit looked tasty, beautiful and eating it would make them wise. But God had already given them access to all knowledge – demonstrated by Adam's ability to name every animal – so Eve wanted what she already had. And we know how that turned out. It is counter intuitive but we have to give up the things we want to keep, confident that we won't lose out, nor will others in our care. But the only way to know this for sure is to try it. **See Practice 21, page 140.**

The Higher Four Levels

Letting go of positive feelings is a precondition to absolute freedom and is a characteristic of those at the higher four levels. It is from the fourth stage of *sattvapati* that the unreality if the material world becomes increasingly evident.

Ramana Maharshi referred to those at each of the four higher levels as *brahmavit* – knowers of Brahman, the Absolute or supreme universal consciousness. He referred to those at four, five, six and seven respectively as *brahmavit* (a knower of Brahman), *brahmavidvara* (more of a knower of Brahman), *brahmavidvariya* (an even better knower of Brahman) and *brahmavid varistha* (the best of the knowers of Brahman). Men and women at each of these stages have experience of the nature and truth of consciousness itself. Those at level four live in the light of *sattva* and shed that light for others; they are courageous and are consciously working for liberation for themselves and others. In fact Ramana Maharshi referred to level four as 'Full Realisation'. In other traditions it is the stage of perfection.

While *sattvapati* partakes of both the lower and higher levels, the next three stages beginning with *asangsakti* start the final part of the journey. Their chief feature is that the aspirant gets more and more insight into the reality of himself and the universe, and he or she begins to see the essentially ephemeral nature of what was hitherto keenly felt to be of the utmost importance. These aspirants come to realise the insubstantiality of that which seemed solid and true – not just closely held opinions and fierce infatuations. These already dropped away at the earlier stages. The higher stages of consciousness bring with them insight into the dreamlike nature of the so-called solid world. Again Shakespeare described the view beyond the appearance of things at *asangsakti:*

Our revels now are ended. These our actors,
As I foretold you, were all spirits and
Are melted into air, into thin air:
And, like the baseless fabric of this vision,
The cloud-capped towers, the gorgeous palaces,
The solemn temples, the great globe itself,
Yea, all which it inherit, shall dissolve
And, like this insubstantial pageant faded,
Leave not a rack behind. We are such stuff
As dreams are made on, and our little life
Is rounded with a sleep.[49]

Just as upon waking a dream is known to have been insubstantial; so *our* world, made up of opinions and beliefs, fears and hopes, anticipations and dread, inaccurate memories and crazy hopes, also disappears.

Love and the *Gunas*

But wait! When this 'real' world disappears what then? Does the awakened sage see a swirling mass of amorphous nothingness? Do we become a sort of zoned-out detached wanderer to whom family and friends mean nothing? Do we work to right wrong and correct injustice – or do we see it all as absolute and therefore OK? The short answer is no, this rather spaced out uncaring condition does not sound appealing. So what does happen when one reaches the higher levels?

Love is the answer, so let us consider love. First let's revisit the *gunas* so we can look at how love appears differently in *tamas*, *rajas* and *sattva*. In the previous chapter we saw that the *gunas* were modalities of consciousness which had an effect on everything. When positive *sattva* is the force of insight, stillness and wakefulness; *rajas* is the power of movement and creativity; and *tamas* is measure and law. When *sattva* – showing itself as reason, insight and intelligence – is in the ascendant all works well; the other *gunas* operate positively – *rajas* as purposeful, focused action; and *tamas* as regulation which knows when to start and when to stop. But when unregulated by *sattva*, *rajas* is unbridled, passionate and often destructive activity; and *tamas* has a deadening effect.

49 William Shakespeare, *The Tempest,* act 4, scene 1, lines 148–158.

In Chapter 18 of the Bhagavad Gita Krishna spends quite some time elucidating the tamasic, rajasic and sattvic aspects of a range of things. In the terms of this analysis *sattva* is the pure quality which conducts the force of consciousness as insight, serenity and intelligence. The other gunas are taken in their uncontrolled aspect. Table 4 is a summary of this analysis:

TABLE 4:

Chapter 18 of the Bhagavad Gita – The *gunas* in context

	Sattvic	**Rajasic**	**Tamasic**
Knowledge	That knowledge which sees unity in diversity.	That knowledge which sees diverse existence and all beings as separate.	That knowledge which clings blindly to one idea, without logic, truth or insight.
Action	Duty done without attachment, with neither like nor dislike, with no thought of reward.	Acts done, even strenuously, for reward, for pleasurable consequences, or done out of egotism.	Acts done out of delusion, without regard for the consequences, or harm, or the ability of the doer.
The Actor/ Doer	A doer free from attachment and egotism, possessed of courage and confidence, unaffected by success and failure.	A doer who is impulsive, greedy, looking for reward, violent, impure, torn between joy and sorrow.	A doer who is unsteady, vulgar, stubborn, deceptive, malicious, lazy, despondent, procrastinating.
Intellect	That intellect which knows action and inaction, and which discriminates between what ought and ought not be done, and between fear and fearless-ness, bondage and freedom.	That intellect which knows neither right from wrong, nor what should and shouldn't be done.	That intellect which is shrouded in ignorance, thinks right wrong, and sees everything perversely.
Conviction	That conviction and steady concentration by which mind, life and the senses are under control.	That conviction which holds to duty and ritual, self-interest and wealth for the sake of their results.	That conviction which clings stupidly to false ideas, fear, grief, despair and lust.
Pleasure	That pleasure which seems, at first, like poison but ends as nectar, e.g. giving up smoking.	That pleasure which delights the senses and seems at first like nectar but ends like poison, e.g. over-eating.	That pleasure which from first to last merely drugs the senses and which springs from lethargy, laziness and folly, e.g. addictions of any sort.

Tamasic love – bondage

The reach of the *gunas* is universal. Love also has three aspects ruled by each of the *gunas*. Starting from the lowest and working our way up, when *tamas* rules, love takes the form of such close identification with the object of our love that when something happens to the beloved, we, the lover, feel it has happened to us. We are elated in the triumphs and destroyed by the disasters of the object of our love. In Sanskrit this is known as *moha*, meaning bondage, loss of consciousness, bewilderment, perplexity, distraction, infatuation, delusion, error, folly.

Grief

Grief is a natural response to great loss – the death of loved ones is the most obvious example. But there is a measure to everything and grief which is all consuming and never ends becomes an emotional prison – like Miss Haversham in *Great Expectations* who, jilted by her lover, wears her torn and decaying wedding dress and lives in a gloomy isolated world of hard-hearted grief.

This is a form of tamasic bondage where we almost literally 'feel the other's pain'. Often we hold on to grief because we feel we will be letting go of the departed loved one, or we think we will betray their memory by 'getting over' their death. This feeling of betrayal is not true. If you could actually ask your dearly departed loved ones if they want you to mourn them for the rest of your life, what do you suppose their answer would be? 'Yes, I believe I was *such* a special person. I feel it would be entirely appropriate that until the day of your death, you should spend every waking moment thinking of me, missing me and grieving for your loss; and you should ignore your living friends and relatives. I could even haunt your dreams.' Any friend or relative worth grieving for would be justifiably horrified if you attributed this attitude to them. And aren't there other people, friends and family, who are still alive and who need your love and attention?

There are compassionate qualified professionals who specialise in grief counselling and who can help ensure that the deceased are remembered, honoured and their memory is cherished without crippling the living. In situations such as this my strong advice is to seek help.

In *tamas*, love takes the form of close identification and bondage, and this *moha* is dissolved by the work done at levels one, two and three. Part of the purification of mind in *tanumanasa* is the dissolution of this type of burdensome ignorance. This leaves us with rajasic and sattvic love. **See Practice 22, page 140.**

Rajasic love – attachment

In *rajas* love appears as *raga* or attachment. *Raga* literally means to dye or colour, and because strong emotion dyes or colours the situation and our attitudes, *raga* comes to mean passion or feeling, infatuation, sympathy, affection. Again, the idea is clear. It means love for another. In the state of attachment we see the beloved as an object external and different from us, essentially we are here and they are over there. If separated from the beloved we yearn to be with them, we want their attention and, usually, we bargain with them. We give a little of our love and in return we want a little (or a lot) of theirs. At level four – *sattvapati* – this rajasic form of love still operates and part of the work at level four is to allow it, and the notion of the creation made up of separate beings and objects, to dissolve and pass away.

Practices 23 and 24 (page 141) address this feeling of being 'other'. These practices can allow us to experience a taste of the state of *asangsakti*. One of the characteristics of this level of *asangsakti* is, in fact, that the rajasic form of love which is based on the concept of otherness has disappeared and all love is sattvic.

Sattvic love – union

There are some similarities between tamasic and sattvic love. Both are unmoving and in a way in both the lover sees himself in the beloved. But while this identification is enslaving in *tamas*, in *sattva* it is liberating. Shanatananda Saraswati points out that in *tamas* love is clouded by ignorance while in *sattva* it is infused with true knowledge.

In love you always give and don't demand in return. By giving, you allow things to happen. … real love means no demands from the beloved.[50]

---

[50] Shantananda Saraswati, *Good Company,* Study Society, 1992, p. 145.

In *sattva*, for example, we see the happiness of the beloved as our happiness and we wish only that the beloved prosper. This identification is liberating rather than binding. This is the form of love which predominates in *asangsakti*.

Enjoying the Glory

In this state of ever-giving love, aware that everything perceived is sourced from limitless consciousness, the person who has reached *asangsakti* experiences and enjoys the brilliance and glory of the creation. They are in a childlike state of wonder at all the astonishing intricacy and beauty of the universe. This is not a naïve, unrealistic state – quite the opposite. Many of the issues which seem serious and important at the lower levels are only deemed to be so by our thinking. This is easy to demonstrate by considering an issue which you *don't* really care about. Perhaps you are not particularly interested in politics. Just observe how each side of any particular political argument is completely and passionately convinced of the rightness of their cause and of the disastrous consequences of the policies of their opponents. And yet *you* can see, regardless of how the argument is resolved, that the world will continue to bump along in reasonably good order.

Those at level five see the wonderful variety and unifying orderly lawfulness of the creation beyond all the conflicts of right and wrong; yes and no; black and white. This is not to say that they are unaware of injustice or mismeasure, but their starting point in finding a remedy is compassion and love for all parties involved in the dispute. **See Practice 25, page 141.**

The Will of the Absolute

One happy spin-off of this ability to delight in every aspect of the universe is to experience events as messages from the universe, sometimes referred to as the 'will of the Absolute'. These messages give direction to one's life, because, when Consciousness itself gives clear directions on how to act or to stop acting it would be a brave, not to say, foolhardy, individual who would ignore it.

A great example of this is in Plato's *Phaedrus*. In this dialogue Socrates and his eponymous interlocutor are discussing the nature of love and after giving an erudite disquisition Socrates stands up to leave. He puts one foot in the Illisus River when his daemon or, as we might call it, his guardian angel warns him to stop as he has offended the god of love by imputing some form of evil or bad intent to him. Socrates returns to Phaedrus and gives a further speech which rectifies the previous error. Socrates received a message from the universe, the will of the Absolute was communicated to him, and he unhesitatingly obeyed.

Whilst anyone at any level can at least begin to appreciate this phenomenon, those at *asangsakti* experience it in such a way that it makes a significant difference in their speech and actions. They see and feel everything that happens as a message from the universal consciousness; they interpret the message reasonably accurately, and they act on it.

Getting the message

At lower levels we generally experience messages as coming from outside ourselves. At the higher levels of consciousness we experience them as coming from inside also. Like Socrates we experience some thoughts or feelings as messages to act or refrain from action; to speak or to remain silent, and so on. The key here is that at *asangsakti* we can sift the useless chatter of the ego from the clear voice of the true Self. This is immensely important because if we mistake the one for the other we can fall into egregious error. Great harm can be done by those who hear the chatter in their heads as the voice of God.

So how can we tell if these promptings are true or false? One good way is to see if they are unifying, exclude no one and work against the ego rather than for it. These inner messages should also line up with indicators from authoritative sources like do unto others; honouring father and mother; not committing adultery; to thine own self be true, and so on. Another tip is to start small so, if you are wrong, not much harm is done. Perfection is not required, just conscientious good intent, and the willingness to learn from mistakes.

As a headmaster I walk around the school on a daily basis and there are sometimes items out of place – and often I get a message to pick something up, wash some coffee cups or tidy up some papers. I try to be vigilant and attend to these small matters because it attunes me to similar promptings when something big is going down. One of the features of these little promptings is that they frequently bring up some minor egoic opposition – 'not enough time', 'it's someone else's job', and so on.

Another example: Before I was married I was driving the short distance home from my wife's flat one night. To get home I had to make a lengthy loop around a one-way system. Or (my preferred option) I could nip the wrong way down a short one-way street and be home in no time. Just as I was entering the street another car came towards me and the driver gave me an earful of abuse. As it happened we had just been hearing Shantananda Saraswati's advice on this idea of accepting the events of life as a series of universal messages. I therefore listened to the vigorous abuse and asked myself: 'What is the message here?' The message I took was not to take short cuts – not just with traffic and driving but as an approach to life. And since then I have tried to adopt this attitude of giving activities, people and projects their due time rather than cutting corners.

Bad things are also messages from a loving universe

At *asangsakti* we see everything which happens as a message from the universe – and further, we see them as loving messages. The Universe is, according to the wise, beneficent. It means only good and not harm. The conscious intelligence which creates, preserves and dissolves the universe and all its parts, is a force of love, mercy and compassion. Now try telling that to someone who has suffered abuse, or bereavement or some other catastrophe (or rather don't). (But see **Practice 26, page 141.**)

A GOOD THING OR A BAD THING?

There is a story which illustrates this: a village bred horses for sale. One day the horses escaped to the mountains, and all the villagers ran to their head man and cried bitterly about their loss. He said: 'You never know whether it is a good thing, or a bad thing.'

Then the horses came back with a pack of brood mares, doubling the village's herd. Again they ran to the head man to tell him, this time proclaiming their good fortune, and again he said: 'You never know whether it is a good thing, or a bad thing.'

Then, when breaking in the new horses the head man's son fell and broke his leg. The villagers were distraught and ran to tell him. Yet again he said: 'You never know whether it is a good thing, or a bad thing.'

When a war broke out all the young men of the village except the head man's son were taken away to fight. The story ends there but the head man's response would still be appropriate.

THE CONVOY

An elderly friend of mine was an aircraft engineer during the Second World War. While in a massive convoy just leaving England for Singapore in 1941, his ship had engine trouble and was ordered to Glasgow for repairs. A good thing, or a bad thing?

The convoy sailed without them. When the ship had been repaired the original crew refused to sail from Glasgow because no seagulls were following the ship and this was a sign that the ship would sink. They finally embarked with a new (and presumably less superstitious) crew. A few days later they were torpedoed off the Azores. Hundreds of men were lost but my friend's lifeboat was rescued and he saw out the war in Africa.

The convoy he was meant to be with made it to Singapore just in time for everyone to be captured by the Japanese. Many of his comrades worked as slave labourers on the Thai–Burma railway.

THE TWO DISCIPLES

Ramakrishna tells of two friends who go to a guru to hear his teaching. One friend does as the guru instructs and keeps going back for further guidance; the other loses interest and instead goes to the red light district of the town. Each morning each of the young men sets out on his journey. The devotee, regardless of how careful he is, invariably steps on a sharp thorn hurting his foot. The other chap, also without fail, finds a single gold coin on the way to the fleshpots. The devotee finally asks his guru why he seems to receive punishment, while his friend receives a reward on his way to riotous living.

The guru explains that each of them is playing out past karma, but this karma has been modified by their respective choices in this lifetime. The devoted young man was fated to suffer horrendous injury but, because he has chosen a path of devotion to truth, this fate had been modified so he merely pricks his foot with a thorn for a few mornings. The other chap was fated to receive untold riches, which had, in turn, been reduced to a few gold coins because of his foolish choice. You don't know whether it is a good thing or a bad thing.

The power to choose

At *asangsakti* we see the wonder and glory of the universe, we see events as messages from the Universe and we heed those messages and grow in wisdom. We are at peace with the ups and downs of life because both are interesting and enjoyable lessons in the real school of life. The practices in this chapter are designed to give you an experience of this fifth stage of the journey. **See Practice 27, page 142.**

At *asangsakti* we are not bound by relationships and events. Easy come, easy go is our motto without being irresponsible or unrealistic. If there *is* anything which binds us it is love for everything we experience – not in the sense of slavery, more that we become a devotee of the Lord as it were in everything. Mother Teresa, for example, always denied that she was helping the poor. Again and again she insisted that she was serving Christ and she saw Him in everyone and everything.

Asangsakti means 'the power of detachment' and this detachment gives us the power to see things as they are and to move freely between the twin poles of right and wrong, good and bad without being pulled by either. At *asangsakti* we are untouched by the cares of the world; we have time and space to make reasonable choices; and we take measured, intelligent steps on the way to freedom.

The binding aspect of tamasic love and the attachment of rajasic love are transformed at *asangsakti* into *prema* – pure, unattached love where the lover and the beloved are on the brink of union. Here is a Zen story illustrating this loving detachment.

IS THAT SO?

The Zen master Hakuin was praised by his neighbours as one living a pure life.

A beautiful Japanese girl whose parents owned a food store lived near him. Suddenly, without warning, her parents discovered she was with child. This made her parents very angry. She would not confess who the man was, but after much harassment at last named Hakuin.

In great anger the parents went to the master. 'Is that so?' was all he would say.

After the child was born it was brought to Hakuin. By this time he had lost his reputation, which did not trouble him, but he took very good care of the child. He obtained milk from his neighbours and everything else the little one needed.

A year later the girl-mother could stand it no longer. She told her parents the truth – that the real father of the child was a young man who worked in the fishmarket.

The mother and father of the girl at once went to Hakuin to ask his forgiveness, to apologise at length, and to get the child back again.

Hakuin was willing. In yielding the child, all he said was: 'Is that so?'

Genesis: The Fifth Day – Fish and Fowl

Asangsakti, the fifth step on the way to freedom and happiness corresponds to the fifth day of creation:

20 *And God said, Let the waters bring forth abundantly the moving creature that hath life, and fowl that may fly above the earth in the open firmament of heaven.*

21 *And God created great whales, and every living creature that moveth, which the waters brought forth abundantly, after their kind, and every winged fowl after his kind: and God saw that it was good.*

22 *And God blessed them, saying, Be fruitful, and multiply, and fill the waters in the seas, and let fowl multiply in the earth.*

23 *And the evening and the morning were the fifth day.*

There are several interesting aspects in this description. First it is the waters, symbolising love, which bring forth the creatures that hath life. Love is the greatest of all creative forces; there is the obvious example of a married couple bringing children into the world and raising them in a loving household. But we can also see this when we create anything. If we work with love the creative act gets our whole attention, we take pains and the product is likely to be beautiful and long lasting. We take care of the details and spare no effort. If we work begrudgingly we are more likely to cut corners and the finished product, while superficially according to plan, will be more likely to be shoddy and second rate. These creatures created from the waters of love move and have life.

Secondly, the creatures move freely and naturally in their proper element. This is the nature of life at the level of *asangsakti*. We move freely in our natural element and so do all our faculties – reason, intelligence, faith, physical prowess. Plato called this free and natural activity Justice – when all our faculties do their job well and don't try to do the job of another. He used the analogy of a republic where we don't ask cobblers to fix our plumbing, we don't ask teachers to pilot our ships and we don't ask shopkeepers to rule our country.

A third aspect of the description of the fifth day is that the creatures are brought forth abundantly. This shows us one of the basic laws of the universe. When the universe gives, it gives with astonishing generosity. Jesus commented on this in relation to wheat where He noted that a single grain grows into an ear bearing sixty to a hundred more seeds. Many of His miracles exemplified this abundance – turning a few loaves and fishes into a meal for thousands. Leon MacLaren in his study of economics pointed out a fundamental error of modern economics which propagates the idea of the uneven division of scarce resources. MacLaren held that the basic law of economics is abundance. Where there is scarcity vested interests, greed or some other artificial blockage has been put in place to the natural flow of plentiful wealth.

Lastly, not only does God decree that the creatures come forth abundantly, after their kind, He gives them His first blessing, saying: Be fruitful, and multiply, and fill the waters in the seas, and let fowl multiply in the earth. They are blessed with God's own creative power so they themselves can 'be fruitful and multiply'. This is illustrative of the creativity, freedom and access to abundance which we enjoy at *asangsakti*, because we in turn have the power to generate this freedom abundantly for others. Having reached this level and realised its qualities of creativity, freedom, abundance we are ready to move to level six.

PRACTICE 21 ➤ ➤ ➤ ➤ ➤ ➤ ➤ ➤

Sit quietly and inwardly still. Remember yourself as the unmoving witnessing consciousness. Remaining at rest, think of anyone or anything you love – spouse, child, friend, pet. Feel love welling up inside you and let it flow freely to the object of your love, and to anyone or anything else in the Universe that could do with a little more love. Seek nothing in return.

Try this exercise with other positive feelings: admiration, courage, fortitude, and so on. Remember the Self within and let the energy of that feeling flow out to whoever needs it. Don't keep any of it back for yourself, and don't look for any pay off.

If you feel peaceful and content as a result of this exercise, send the energy of those feelings out as well to whomever in the world needs a little peace right at this moment.

Now: do you feel depleted or fuller?

PRACTICE 22 ➤ ➤ ➤ ➤ ➤ ➤ ➤ ➤

I can't better Brandon Bays's Journey work or the Sedona Method of releasing, devised by Lester Levenson, of releasing when dealing with deep emotions such a grief, anger and resentment – sometimes lasting years. My strong recommendation is to explore some of these techniques or seek counselling if you have some unresolved issues which you feel are holding you back.

One thing you might like to try is to rest and become quiet and, when you can trust yourself to be a little detached and objective, summon your image of the lost loved one, or the offending party and have as open, compassionate and truthful conversation as possible with them. Tell them exactly how you feel and let 'them' reply. This is a part of Brandon Bays's System – the whole of her process is marvellously liberating. You might note Jesus's advice to 'Forgive them, for they know not what they do', realising that most people who hurt us have very little idea of the effect they have on us.

On this, as on so many other similar topics, the Sedona Method has practical life affirming techniques which can help people move on in a compassionate and empowering way.

PRACTICE 23 ➤ ➤ ➤ ➤ ➤ ➤ ➤ ➤ ➤

This is a practice adapted from one given to us in the School of Philosophy.

Rest in the presence of yourself as witness, and let the mind fall still and be at peace. Allow the senses to receive impressions. Note whether these impressions and objects and sensations are experienced as being other than yourself. If so ask yourself this question: 'Where do I end, and where does "other" begin?'

Get a sense of where this dividing line between you and other is, and allow that demarcation line gently to dissolve and disappear. Let go of the idea of other. Don't get lost in feelings of unity, just let go of feelings of separation.

And rest in that feeling without naming or labelling it.

PRACTICE 24 ➤ ➤ ➤ ➤ ➤ ➤ ➤ ➤ ➤

Rest in the presence of yourself as witness, and let the mind fall still and be at peace. Allow the senses to receive impressions.

Note the feeling of 'other' in yourself. Experience the feeling of yourself as other than the people and objects around you. Let the feeling go, just let it dissolve.

We are not trying to establish unity, we just release the feeling of our own otherness.

PRACTICE 25 ➤ ➤ ➤ ➤ ➤ ➤ ➤ ➤ ➤

Think of an issue which riles you (political, environmental, domestic or professional). Bring to mind the participants who aggravate you, or have opposing views, or who are acting unjustly or unreasonably. With their picture in your mind say to them: 'I love you.' Repeat this until it's true.

PRACTICE 26 ➤ ➤ ➤ ➤ ➤ ➤ ➤ ➤ ➤

After some minor setback – a lost wallet, a scratched car, a disappointing mark in a test – ask 'What can I learn from this event?' Being more awake so the wallet doesn't go missing, parking more carefully or studying harder. But also, perhaps, accepting events cheerfully, remembering those less fortunate than you (without a wallet, car or university place).

PRACTICE 25 ➤ ➤ ➤ ➤ ➤ ➤ ➤ ➤ ➤

Think of a situation which provokes a negative emotional reaction in you. It might be a situation which is irritating or makes you impatient or jealous.

Now imagine that you are someone else. You are now a person who just doesn't have the internal buttons which this situation pushes, who shrugs their shoulders and can't see what all the fuss is about. You are now this other person. Just for a few moments feel the freedom of not caring at all.

Now, bring 'yourself' back and feel the way you usually do. Immerse yourself in those familiar feelings of irritation and stress. Now switch back again and become the other, indifferent person. Take the time to really be that other person. Repeat this back and forth shift a few more times, make sure you really feel each part you are playing.

This exercise shows you that you can in fact choose how you respond to the world. You might like to take this practice 'on the road' and become free and indifferent at the time the provocative situation is actually happening.

One warning: this practice is not meant to make you unresponsive when action or words are called for. Quite the opposite. This exercise can free you from the emotional clutter which covers the appropriate response.

•   •   •   •   •   •   •

Chapter **Six**

Step Six: Non-Awareness of Separate Objects

CASE STUDY A PERSONAL EXAMPLE

It was once suggested to me that I might try sitting still for a couple of days; to have meals and sleep at night, but for the rest of the time simply to sit without moving. I followed this advice and sat for about five hours in the morning and a similar period in the afternoon. My main effort was not to 'do' anything – no physical movement, of course, but also no mantra or other mental activity. Every hour or so I stretched but otherwise I just sat upright and comfortably with my eyes closed. I kept the movements of my mind under observation and kept letting go of any thoughts or feelings. I followed this regime for two days.

On the afternoon of the second day I was falling asleep when, in my mind, I heard a voice telling me in no uncertain terms to get my act together, focus my attention and re-establish the discipline. I was jolted out of sleep and with this renewed focus I was suddenly bathed in a warm, bright, golden light. It was joyful and energising. Rather than trying to hold on to it, however, I just observed the light, and didn't get hooked on it.

The light faded and, at that moment, sitting unmoving with my eyes closed, it was as if a door against which I was leaning gently opened and I felt like I was falling backwards into darkness. As I sank deeper and deeper into this darkness I felt limitlessly blissful. It was a feeling of contentment and timelessness. When the sensation of falling ceased I was suspended in consciousness as a point of existence only. I had no body-consciousness at all. In that condition the only reasonable thing to do was to sing the praises of the Absolute and to rest in the ineffable peace. I was conscious of my own individual existence but with no ganglia of body or mind or ego. And I was completely content to rest in that timeless condition. I knew myself to be separate from the limitless consciousness, but felt no need to make any effort or apply any discipline to unite with it. It was as if I was waiting for the Absolute Himself to invite me into complete union.

After about half an hour I emerged from this state and became aware that I was in my body again. This state of *samadhi* has shown itself repeatedly since then, less fully but still recognisably, in meditation and also during the day's activities when I remember to rest inwardly.

Padarthabhavani

The sixth stage on the way to complete freedom and happiness is known in Sanskrit as *padarthabhavani*. At this stage we experience our individual existence, while perceiving everything else as a single blissful unity. We see no differences between diverse forms, creatures or beings. Sound familiar? It should, because this state is more common than we may think.

Consider the way in which many of us start on the spiritual quest. Often it is with an experience of profound awakening. Perhaps we felt infinitely great and our usual sense of self disappeared; or we felt a connection with everything around us, or the scene took on an unusual clarity and was bathed in light. Experiences such as these, even if fleeting, are often accompanied by a sense of peace and complete contentment – we have nowhere to go, nothing to do and nothing to achieve; the whole universe is experienced as a single unified consciousness. For that brief instant we are completely desireless. And the memory of this moment stays with us for the rest of our lives. This is the experience of *padarthabhavani*.

In this state our perception of the world outside us changes. We cease to see or experience separate forms. At level six we feel our own individual existence, and perceive everything else, 'other', as a singularity, bound in a relationship of pure love. While at *asangsakti* we also experience love for everything, we see forms and people as differentiated from ourselves and from each other.

SUKA AND THE BATHERS

In the Mahabharata there is a story of Suka the son of Vyasa. Suka was walking on a river bank when he came across some women bathing. As Suka passed, the women rose from the water to worship him regardless of their state of undress. Vyasa, the holy sage who was the author of the Mahabharata and himself a man of high consciousness, was following Suka along the river bank. When Vyasa came in sight, the women hastily adjusted their clothing. He was puzzled and asked why they had done this when they hadn't seemed concerned by Suka. They replied that Suka saw only God everywhere and had no sense of difference of forms including, of course, differences related to sex and gender. Vyasa, they said, although a perfected sage, was still conscious that they were women, and so they modestly covered themselves in his presence.

Samadhi

In this story Suka has his senses turned outwards. But this state of *padarthabhavani* is often experienced in deep meditation when one leaves the world behind and enters the state of consciousness known as *samadhi*. The state of *samadhi* is one of focused and concentrated attention. On attaining this state we transcend the usual mix of confusion, doubt, desire and aversion which abound at the lower stages of the journey to freedom. Meditation, at its most effective, takes us gently into *samadhi*, but it can also be attained as the fruit of other spiritual disciplines. **See Practice 28, page 156.**

THE ARROW MAKER

A disciple went to a village to obtain provisions for the ashram. He was just passing the shop of an arrow maker when a wedding procession with its colourful display and loud music and singing went by. He asked the arrow maker about the wedding. The arrow maker looked up from his work and said he hadn't been aware of the procession as he had had his whole attention on the point of the arrow.

Concentration: Art Appreciation

Sometimes we can enter this state of *padarthabhavani* through concentrated attention on a task before us.

On our travels my wife and I have visited many museums and galleries to experience the iconic master works of artistic greatness and ingenuity; but we found that by trying to drink everything in we got a sort of experiential indigestion. We got to a point where if we saw one more Madonna and Child we would scream. The gift and coffee shop looked ever more alluring. So we decided to adopt another policy. We would go and spend time with just one master work.

When we were in Paris we went to see the Mona Lisa. On arrival we sat in front of it and just let our eyes rest on it. My approach was to give attention rather than seek to get any 'experience' from the painting. The picture is so familiar that at first it was hard to 'see' it at all. I could only see my ideas and associations. But after some time in quiet contemplation, and by letting these blocking ideas go, I received a jolt of energy, insight and knowledge; I seemed for an instant to enter the painting. This energy sent me spinning off and I then spent a further ten minutes or so getting over this experience so I could again connect with the painting.

Gradually the painting came alive and this time it gently drew me into a deep world of peace, knowledge and beauty. It began to reveal itself as a window into the realm of feminine power, love and creativity. It was like seeing and experiencing the universal force we call Mother Nature with its infinite potential and creative possibilities. I felt its power to nurture, support and protect every creature, and to do all this effortlessly, without judgment and without asking or requiring anything for herself. I was aware of myself in this act of contemplation but my attention was wholly absorbed in the picture, nothing else – time, other tourists – existed for me.

After some time resting in this blissful substance I knew it was time to go. Any more would have been greedy. When I get the opportunity I contemplate a master work in this way – sitting quietly giving it my attention and letting go of any desire to get anything from it. I find about half an hour seems to suit me. **This is Practice 29, page 156.**

Padarthabhavani and 'Flow'

Modern psychologists have discovered *padarthabhavani*. The educational psychologist Mihály Csíkszentmihályi (pronounced Meehi Chikshent-meehi) calls this state 'flow' and has popularised it in his seminal work *Flow: The Psychology of Optimal Experience.*[51] He defined 'flow' as 'being completely involved in an activity for its own sake. The ego falls away. Time flies. Every action, movement, and thought follows inevitably from the previous one, like playing jazz. Your whole being is involved, and you're using your skills to the utmost.'[52] This is very like a description of *samadhi*.

Psychologists identify two types of motivation: extrinsic, when something is done for a reward – money, love, praise and so on – and is therefore sourced from outside; and intrinsic motivation, when the reward is inherent in the doing of the task for its own sake; there is no reason for the action other than the performance of the task itself. Flow is a complete form of intrinsic motivation.

Flow is characterised by a sense of timelessness, contentment, peace and freedom. Those who experience it speak of knowing precisely what to do and of having all the time in the world. Sportsmen and athletes speak of it as being 'in the zone'. Skilled craftsmen, singers and actors, or just ordinary folk who slip unheralded into a state of present awareness, are in this state of flow. I find it when teaching children, studying history or speaking to large audiences (go figure).

Flow involves work that is not too easy or too hard. Csíkszentmihályi

---

[51] Harper Perennial, New York 1991.

[52] Wired Magazine, September, 1996, http://www.wired.com/wired/archive/4.09/czik.html

said work which is too easy lacks challenge, making the task boring and allowing the mind to wander. At the same time the task should not be too difficult and therefore beyond the skill of the performer of the task. This creates tension and stress which keeps the mind from entering the zone.

Follow-ups on Csíkszentmihályi's work have found that meditation, yoga, martial arts and other similar pursuits that require concentration assist their practitioners in finding flow in their daily activities. These pursuits give physical and mental focus and this enters into other areas of life. This state of flow, where the actor is wholly focused on the action for its own sake with no extrinsic motivation, is another form of *padarthabhavani*.

Padartha

Padarthabhavani is a compound made up of *pada, artha* and *abhavani. Pada* means a step or foot – in fact our English word 'foot' is ultimately derived from *pada;* like the Greek *podos* (hence 'podiatry') and the Latin *pes, pedis* (hence 'pedal', 'pedestrian'). *Pada* also means 'measuring out something into even lengths', like a verse or measured unit of sound; and hence it also means 'word' or 'name'. *Artha* means 'sense' or 'significance'. It comes from the root form *arth,* one meaning of which is 'to point out the sense of', or 'to comment upon'. So the compound *padartha* means 'that which corresponds to the meaning of a word, a thing, material object, man or person.' *Padartha,* in the context of *padarthabhavani,* means the essential sound or true inner name of anything in creation.

The causal form

Vedic philosophy holds that everything exists in name and form only. According to this idea everything has an inner essential 'sound'; first comes the sound or name, then the form. According to this view the entire universe, and all its constituent elements, can be perceived as sounds which are bodied forth into perceptible forms. This inner essence of sound or name is therefore sometimes referred to as the causal form of a thing because it comes first and is the cause of the shape that follows. This causal form is beyond the reach of the physical senses and the outer aspects of the mind. It is accessible through a rarefied inner listening, involving an intuitive journey from the outer manifestation to the inner truth of any object – a journey from its outer form to its essential inner sound. In effect it is a form of meditation on the object with a refined subtle listening which reveals the knowledge of its inner essence. At *padarthabhavani* we experience this causal world of subtle sounds and names.

How does this presence of the causal level show itself? Take an everyday example: someone we know might have a tendency to become disproportionately angry at small challenges, setbacks and imagined slights. Friends might seek to persuade this irascible chap that he is jumping at shadows, that these insults and confrontations are only in his imagination. But regardless of this good advice he continues to blow his stack for no real reason. The cause of his tendency to anger is not sourced in objective reality. More likely he is unknowingly listening to a subconscious sentence such as 'I am worthless' or 'I am under attack', and he has developed a hair-trigger response to events and people who (to him) confirm this view.

I was once at a residential retreat. We were practising working under discipline and later I was reporting back to the group about my experiences. I said I had felt competitive and keen to succeed and do better than others. As I was speaking I realised this wasn't entirely accurate. It wasn't really a desire to succeed, but a fear of failure which drove me on. The tutor then asked me why I feared failure. Without any conscious thought a voice (mine) said: 'Because I am a failure.' I had no previous idea that this sentence was running in my subconscious. It was a moment of liberation, because, once stated openly, this governing causal sentence had no more power. Afterwards I began to see that my impulse to criticise others, to compete and succeed, the need to continually prove myself, to dislike having my mistakes pointed out and to overreact to criticism, was all based on this governing sentence – I am a failure. And these reactions had the effect of hiding that sentence from me. Having heard it I began to see it gradually loosen its grip. What a relief!

Another example: I have taught children who seem fearful and diffident, regardless of the encouragement and support they are given by parents and teachers and friends. One aspect of our curriculum is compulsory involvement each year in a Shakespeare play. One of the many reasons for doing this is to allow the children to experience another 'sound' – to be Hamlet or Henry V or Portia. And also to transcend the limiting sentences they may be listening to by working with the rest of the cast; and not least, to step over the natural stage fright and pre-performance nerves that most of us are subject to. In short, the performance is designed to get into that realm of causal sentences and replace a few of the negative ones – 'I can't do this', 'Everyone will laugh at me', 'I'm no good' – with positive experience.

So *padartha* – the meaning of words and things – refers to the realm of causal 'words'. Ultimately the most causal word of all is The Word by which all individual forms are brought into manifestation. After all, according to Genesis, God spoke the universe into existence – God said let there be light. St John tells us that in the beginning was the Word. When Jesus offered to come to cure the centurion's servant, the centurion knew the visit was unnecessary. Jesus had to 'speak the word only, and my servant shall be healed'.[53] According to this doctrine we are all embodied names, and if we can attune our subtle hearing to these sounds and names we would hear the universe continuously singing itself into existence. And these words are bodied forth out of airy nothing and given a local habitation and a name.[54]

A flower

This causal sound or name binds the essence of anything to its outer form. For good or ill you are listening to the sound of 'you' right now and it creates every part of your existence and experience.

As a practical illustration of this we could contemplate a flower. What is it that gives every flower that ever existed, exists now and will exist in the future a common essential feature which makes it a flower and differentiates it from other things? What essentially, is a flower?

Via the senses we will see its colour and shape, we might smell its scent, feel its texture and, if we are so inclined, we can even taste it. If in contemplating all these we ask, 'What, in truth, is a flower?' None of these sensory impressions individually, or even all of them together, are the flower. Some essential 'flowerness' remains elusive. Perhaps we might consider its function as the reproductive organ of the plant. But again,

---

[53] Matthew 8.8.

[54] William Shakespeare, *A Midsummer Night's Dream,* act 5, scene 1.

this reduces a flower to a mechanistic process – which hardly explains the affection and admiration that a young man shyly handing over a bunch on a first date intends to convey. Then what about the beauty, freshness and charm of the flower? Here we are getting a little closer to the essential character.

The key here is to engage the heart as well as the mind and to enter into the being of the flower. Then we transcend the outer form of the flower and its functionality and we experience its vitality, abundance, exuberance and beauty; we can feel the flower as part of the creative force of nature seeking to reproduce and proclaim itself. Then we are getting close to the essential nature of a flower. It is said that this *padartha*, the essential 'is-ness' of the flower, is audible to the inner subtle ear. Jesus spoke of it: 'They who have ears to hear, let them hear.' Shakespeare described it: 'Such harmony is in immortal souls.' Mozart heard it. In describing how he could hear an entire symphony as a single sound, he said: 'What a delight this is, I cannot tell!'

Abhavani

Bhavani is the act of perceiving, ascribing meaning, imagining, fancying, forming a conception in the mind. And *a-bhavani* is the opposite. The *a* is a negative prefix as in theist/atheist; gnostic/agnostic; typical/atypical. So *abhavani* means – not perceiving or ascribing meaning; or, more accurately, transcending separate, individual meanings.

Those whose hearing is attuned to the inner essential sound – the true name of all creatures – hear an exquisite celestial harmony. At *padarthabhavani* the aspirant has transcended the individual sounds and, instead hears a single universal song. When I fell into *samadhi* I went beyond the consciousness of individual forms and I joined this universal song by singing the praises of God, the Absolute universal consciousness.

It is the final part of this compound word – *abhavani* – which gives us the hint, because *padarthabhavani* means *not* ascribing significance or meaning to separate objects of the senses, the mind or heart. Prior to attaining this condition we are aware of separate objects and can hear their essential names; we experience the universe as a glorious symphony of harmonious sounds. In *padarthabhavani* this refined condition is transcended. The separate sounds or words or names which give individual existence to everything lose their appeal, lustre and significance and we hear and see everything as consciousness only.

Seeing the Multitudes ...

Prior to attaining the state of *padarthabhavani* we see separate objects and creatures; afterwards this perception of multiplicity drops away and we see and hear unity. In the opening verses of the Beatitudes Matthew describes these two conditions:

> *And seeing the multitudes, he went up into a mountain: and when he was set, his disciples came unto him: And he opened his mouth, and taught them, saying ...*[55]

Jesus was in a state where He perceived differences between objects – He saw the multitudes. This is quite a useful state for moving in and responding to the world in general. But when it came time to teach His inner circle of disciples He 'went up into a mountain' or, in other words, He attained an even higher state of consciousness. A mountain, which is wide at the base and narrows to a small single point, is often used as a symbol of spiritual ascent (or descent, depending on the direction). When Jesus was established at this high point then His disciples also made the ascent, and it was then that He could communicate the nine blessings which we now know as the Beatitudes. Jesus established Himself at a point where He no longer saw a multitude, He was no longer ascribing significance to separate objects. This is the state of *padarthabhavani*. It is clear therefore that the Beatitudes (blessed are the meek, and so on) came directly from a particularly refined level of consciousness.

Genesis: The Sixth Day – Animals and Man

So what of the sixth day of creation? How does it relate to *padarthabhavani*? Quite a lot happens on this day and it is well worth looking at it in detail. God commands the earth to bring forth living creatures – cattle, creeping things and beasts. The text emphasises that these creatures are made 'after

---

[55] Matthew 5:1, 2.

their kind'. In other words creatures reproduce other like creatures. It is after all convenient that, say, a crocodile egg contains a baby crocodile, and a swan gives birth to more swans. A certain consistency, not to say, inertia, is therefore built into the creation.

Taken subtly this means that love gives rise to love, anger to anger, and so on. As you sow, so shall you reap. As we have seen, in the causal realm certain sounds, names and sentences govern our thoughts, feelings and actions – they bring forth creatures 'after their kind'. 'I don't deserve to be loved' produces a life which confirms this crazy idea. At *padarthabhavani* we have an understanding of this creative power of causal sound and we can begin to choose what sound we will listen to: 'I am a failure' or 'I am pure, perfect and complete'.

And God saw that the generation of creatures after their kind was good, that is, it was as it should be. There is justice in things flowing from their causes. If greed produced happiness, if compassion led to suffering, or if violence resulted in love, then there would be no justice, and no incentive to cleave to a path of *dharma* or lawful living.

This emphasis on the lawful justice of the creation sets the scene for the appearance of Man, the culmination of created beings. The creation of Man is unique because only here does God say: Let us make man in our image, after our likeness. What does this reference to an image mean? Leon Kass points out that an image such as a photograph is both like and unlike its original. I have a photograph of my wife in my wallet. If I were to show it I would say: 'This is my wife.' The photo points to and reminds me of the original, and couldn't exist without the original, but it is not in fact my wife.[56]

Like that photo Man, made in God's image, resembles and reminds us of God, but, at this stage, at level six, he has not yet become God. This point is subtly reinforced because man is made on the same day as the earth-dwelling creatures. Man is like God but also earthbound. This dichotomy is symbolised in mythology by creatures like the sphinx, the centaur and others with the lower body of an animal and the upper body of a human. Our lower nature is subject to animal urges which need to be ruled by the higher part which has the power of love and reason. Man is

---

[56] L Kass, *The Beginning of Wisdom: Reading Genesis,* Simon & Schuster, 2003, p. 37.

'the place where the falling angel meets the rising ape.'[57] At level six we haven't yet achieved complete freedom; here vigilance is still required.

After making Man in His image God gives him dominion over the fish, birds and animals and over all the earth. The creatures and the earth symbolise the whole manifest creation — moving and unmoving. Man, at this level, is approaching a state of omnipotence. Of course, this dominion is not tyranny but a lawful and compassionate rule – a sort of trusteeship. As an image of God, man at this level partakes in the solicitude and care that God has for His creation.

So God created man in his own image,
In the image of God created he him;
Male and female created he them.[58]

This creation of man is beyond gender. It includes both the male and the female qualities in the one being. What are these male and female qualities? While it is male to protect, it is female to nurture; male to reason, female to intuit; male to contextualise and extrapolate, female to see detail, nuance and derive immediate meaning. And before accusations of stereotyping start flying, remember – 'male and female created he them'. All of us have both male and female characteristics in different measures, and all of us can learn to balance these qualities by learning from each other. In opposition these male and female qualities are endlessly destructive, but as a partnership they are limitlessly creative and powerful. So male and female created he them; at level six these powers are available – to men and women both.

At this stage God gives Man the same blessing of natural increase that the creatures received: be fruitful and multiply and replenish the earth. And He then instructs them to subdue the earth and to have dominion over the creatures. One of the subtle meanings of this second blessing is that men and women have the power of *self* control; they can exert self-discipline over their earthly faculties. It is the blessing of self-control and empowerment. And it also implies a responsibility to use those powers to restrain unbridled negative forces.

---

[57] T Pratchett, *Hogfather,* p. 270.

[58] Genesis 1:27.

But wait! After God made Man He didn't 'see it was good.' Is this just a stylistic oversight? Or can we infer that man is *not* good? Kass makes the interesting point that the word 'good' in this context does not mean morally sound, but rather complete, finished and fit for its task.[59] Man, according to this interpretation, is not yet complete, and the rest of the Bible is the record of his efforts, his successes and failures to attain completion, wholeness and ultimate sanctity. By implication this is the blessing (sometimes the curse) of free will.

After having created animals and Man, God lays down the proper food for all creatures. Plants and fruits which bear seeds are specifically reserved for mankind, while green herbs are given to the lower creatures. The symbolism of the 'seed' is clear. Part of man's food is that potent, fructifying element which brings forth new life. He is indeed made in God's image with dominion and the power to create new life and forms.

And, finally, God saw every thing that He had made and, behold, it was very good.

The Lonely Seventh Day

One interesting way of interpreting the first six days of creation is to divide them into two sets of three (see Table 5): days one, two and three represent the causal, fixed and unmoving form of, respectively light and dark, space and water, earth and food. Days four, five and six show us these elements in their moving, creative form: heavenly lights, fish and birds, animals and man.

TABLE 5: The Days of Creation Paired Up

Causal, Fixed, Essential	Active, Moving, Increasingly Free
1. Light	**4.** Heavenly lights
2. Firmament separating the waters	**5.** Fish and fowl
3. Earth and plants	**6.** Animals and man

[59] Kass, op. cit., p. 39.

But the seventh day doesn't seem to have a partner. According to the Rabbis the companion to the seventh day – the sanctified Sabbath with its commandment to rest – is the remainder of the Bible, which sets out the means by which this part of God's plan is made manifest, and which provides a path for man to find his way back to unity and fulfilment. This unity and fulfilment is known in Sanskrit as *turiya* – the subject of our next chapter.

PRACTICE 28 ➤ ➤ ➤ ➤ ➤ ➤ ➤ ➤

Many readers of this book will already have been introduced to or initiated into a formal system of meditation. Or you will have come across various practices, such as those outlined previously, which give similar access to inner peace. If not, it is probably time to find a system which suits you, and to take it up. If you already have such a system but, as can happen, it is not being practised regularly, then I suggest you reinvigorate the practice.

I practise meditation on a mantra for half an hour every morning and every evening. Occasionally (say, a couple of times a fortnight) I might shorten the period of meditation because of an unusual schedule, but it is rare that I don't meditate twice a day. Sometimes I will meditate for longer or practice other mind-stilling exercises, but the formal practice of half an hour's meditation is the basis of my daily rest in pure being.

The discipline of sticking to a valid authoritative system regardless of the particular promptings of the mind or ego is itself a powerful means of cleansing the being and orientating yourself towards the truth.

PRACTICE 29 ➤ ➤ ➤ ➤ ➤ ➤ ➤ ➤

Try the concentration activity set out on pages 146–147 when you find yourself in the presence of a great work of art – painting, music, literature. And give yourself the time to give yourself to it.

· · · · · · ·

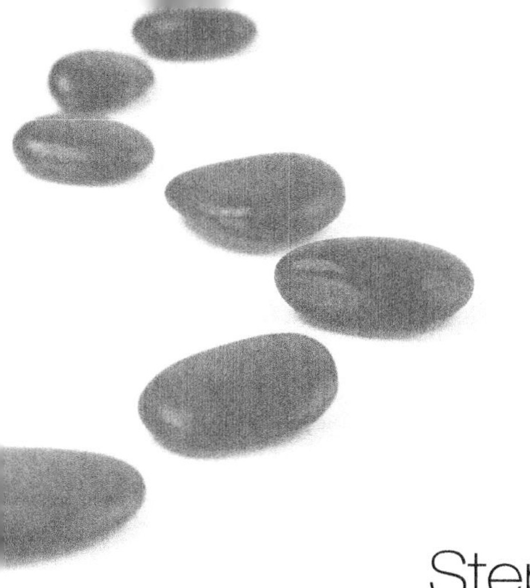

Chapter **Seven**

Step Seven:
Full Realisation of Unity

CASE STUDIES

Buddha: You cannot travel the path until you have become the path itself.

Khalil Gibran: I existed from all eternity and, behold, I am here; and I shall exist till the end of time, for my being has no end.

Baha'u'llah: So powerful is the light of unity that it can illuminate the whole earth.

Byron Katie: I am never unhappy, you can achieve that as well.

Eckhardt Tolle: Having access to that formless realm is truly liberating: it frees you from bondage to form and identification with form. It is life in its undifferentiated state prior to its fragmentation into multiplicity. … It is a realm of deep stillness and peace, but also of joy and intense aliveness. You realise that the light is not separate from who you are but constitutes your very essence.

Moses: Hear O Israel, the Lord our God, the Lord is One.

Plato: In the heaven which is above the heavens, there abides the very being with which true knowledge is concerned: the colourless, formless, intangible essence, visible only to mind, the pilot of the soul. The divine intelligence, being nurtured upon mind and pure knowledge, and the intelligence of every soul.

Jesus: I and the Father are one.

Turiya

The final stage of the seven steps to freedom and happiness is called *turiya* and is a condition in which we know ourselves to be pure impersonal spirit without any taint of limitation or separation. This is the realisation that the individual Self *is* the limitless Absolute or, in Sanskrit, that the *atman* is the Brahman. The term *turiya* is derived from the word for 'four' as it is considered the fourth condition after deep sleep, dreaming and waking. In reality, however, it is not a state because it contains the other three states; it is not just one of the seven steps to freedom as it contains the other six steps.

Turiya is indeed hard to describe because all descriptions imply some limit or differentiation. If it is described as still, it seems to exclude movement; if peaceful it excludes agitation; if expansive it excludes contraction; if it is purity, it seems to exclude impurity; if it is existence then it excludes non-existence. In fact *turiya* contains everything and excludes nothing; it is the diver, the depth and the act of diving; the knower, the known and the act of knowing all in one, without differentiation. Adam and Eve excluded themselves from this unity by heeding the serpent and choosing the differentiated knowledge of good and evil.

Turiya is limitless and universal being-ness. The wise tell us that we are omnipotent, omniscient, omnipresent, and in *turiya* this is known to be true; we cease to believe ourselves to be other than who we truly are.

But *turiya* is virtually impossible to expound, explain or systematise because the words themselves provoke and nail us to some limited form of body, mind or heart. Even descriptions of our limitless being can be externalised into a sort 'Superman' Self – up in the sky! Is it a bird? Is it a plane? This perfect Self becomes externalised (because we know how crummy *we* are) and in turn becomes an object to be attained after long struggle. And for every rung of the ladder we climb a further rung is added at the top making this Self forever unattainable. The General Confession in the Book of Common Prayer tells us that 'We have left undone those things which we ought to have done; and we have done those things which we ought not to have done; and there is no health in us; but thou, O Lord, have mercy upon us miserable offenders.' No wonder these miserable offenders can never reach this God in the sky.

But in *turiya* we know ourselves to be pure, perfect and complete. And we know everything else is as well. It is said that the sages at this level serve by meditating on perfection. Some formulate their knowledge in order to teach those who yearn to be free. In order to teach and guide and formulate instruction those at the highest level need to descend a level or two to connect with the condition of duality in which aspirants find themselves. The compassion and sacrifice of such a move is breathtaking!

Subtle Explanations

Before realisation dawns, *turiya* seems impossible to attain; once it is attained nothing could be simpler or more obvious. The inscrutability of Zen Koans, the gnomic smile of the Mona Lisa, the strange emptiness of the Holy of Holies, Elijah's still, small voice; the rest on the Sabbath day; the unknowable depth of the Upanishads; these are all attempts to bring us to an understanding of the incomprehensible; to explain the inexplicable; to expound the inexpressible.

FACT BOX The Upanishads Come to the West

The story of how the first European translation of the Upanishads became available in 1801 is one of almost impossible coincidence and chance. Several of the Muslim Mughal rulers of India in the 1500s, such as Akbar and Shah Jehan, who built the Taj Mahal as a mausoleum for his favourite wife, had Hindu mothers and wives, and were strikingly tolerant of other religions. Dara Shikoh, the eldest son of Shah Jehan, was, for example, imbued with Sufi mysticism, studied with Christian and Hindu priests and arranged for the Upanishads to be translated into Persian. He believed the Upanishads were the 'secret book' referred to in the Koran.

Dara Shikoh was Shah Jehan's designated successor. Fundamentalist Muslims, taking fright, encouraged his younger brother Aurungzeb to rebel. Dara Shikoh was defeated and beheaded, Aurungzeb ascended the throne and Shah Jehan was imprisoned for the rest of his life. The Mughal dynasty fell into decrepitude soon thereafter and Dara Shikoh's Persian translation of the Upanishads was soon forgotten.

A century and a half later one of the great, unsung heroes of the grand journey of wisdom from East to West, Abraham Hyacinth Auquetil-Duperron went to India in the mid-1700s to find the timeless wisdom which was then thought to be found in the teachings of Zoroaster. As the adherents of Zoroastrianism were thin on the ground in Muslim Persia, Auquetil-Duperron sought out the Zoroastrians of India, known as Parsees. They were reluctant to divulge their sacred texts so in effect he became a

Parsee and wandered through India for seven years before being entrusted with the Zoroastrian texts.

Auquetil-Duperron returned to France and translated them to general dismay as they revealed nothing more than rather mechanistic forms of fire worship. He was even accused of being a charlatan and of foisting on the world a poor forgery. Some years later a French soldier returning from service in India sought our Auquetil-Duperron because of his expertise in Indian languages. The officer had picked up a Persian book in a bazaar, which turned out to be Dara Shikoh's Persian translation of the Upanishads.

During the upheavals of revolution and war in his native France, and afflicted by grinding poverty, Auquetil-Duperron translated it into Latin and French and saw it published in 1801, making them available in the West for the first time in history. Scholars immediately recognised their profound wisdom. [60]

The Upanishads are especially full of mysterious language describing the indescribable. Here is the Kena Upanishad:

Eye, tongue, cannot approach it nor mind know; not knowing we cannot satisfy enquiry. It lies beyond the known, beyond the unknown.[61]

And the Katha Upanishad tells us:

The Self is lesser than the least, greater than the greatest. He lives in all hearts. When senses are at rest, free from desire, Man finds him and mounts beyond sorrow.

Though sitting, He travels; though sleeping, is everywhere …

Who knows the Self, bodiless among the embodied, unchanging among the changing, prevalent everywhere, goes beyond sorrow.

The Self is not known through discourse, splitting of hairs, learning however great; He comes to the man He loves; takes that man's body for His own …

No eye can see Him, nor has He a face that can be seen, yet through meditation and through discipline He can be found in the heart. He that finds Him enters immortal life.

---

[60] S Tathagatananda, *Journey of the Upanishads to the West,* Advaita Ashrama, Kolkata, 2002, p.182ff.

[61] *Ten Principal Upanishads,* op. cit., p.19.

> *When mind and senses are at rest, when the discrimination of intellect is finished, man comes to his final condition.* [61]

The knowledge of the path to *turiya* is not confined to Eastern teachings. Here is a passage from the Philokalia quoted by Edward Gibbon in his *Decline and Fall of the Roman Empire*:

> *When thou art alone in thy cell, shut thy door, and seat thyself in a corner: raise thy mind above all things vain and transitory; recline thy beard and chin on thy breast; turn thine eyes and thy thought towards the middle of thy belly, the region of the navel; and search the place of the heart, the seat of the soul. At first all will be dark and comfortless; but if you persevere day and night, you will feel an ineffable joy; and no sooner has the soul discovered the place of the heart, than it is involved in a mystic and ethereal light.*

(And just to show that you can lead a horse to water but you can't make him drink Gibbon, the child of the 'Enlightenment', calls this beautiful description 'the production of a distempered fancy, the creature of an empty stomach and an empty brain'.) [63]

Para

This area of the navel mentioned in the above quotation is known, in the system of *Shabda Brahman* as *para* – the seat of the Brahman (the Absolute, limitless consciousness) in the body. This is why, in meditation our attention will often naturally settle there, and we can find ourselves like the monks of Mt Athos, gently drawn into a world or pure consciousness by simply dropping below the surface activity of the mind and heart and resting our attention on *para*. We can reduce our identification with the body by resting our attention there when walking, talking or otherwise going about our daily activities.

The other three points in the *Shabda Brahman* system are *pashyanti*, the solar plexus, where Creative Desire sits; *madhyama*, a space below the larynx of ten finger's width, which is the seat of Mind and where the

[62] ibid. pp. 31, 37.

[63] E Gibbon, *The Decline and Fall of the Roman Empire,* vol. VI, Everyman, New York, 1910, p. 265.

Consciousness from *para* and the Creative Desire of *pashyanti* are formulated into speech and thought, and where we can discriminate before we articulate or act. This articulation takes place on the tongue and is known as *waikhari*. **See Practice 30, page 174.**

The Progression to Freedom Through the Six Days of Creation

The description of the Sabbath day in Genesis holds wonderful insight into *turiya*. Before we look at it in depth let's review the first six days and see the progression to the final state of full enlightenment.

The first chapter of Genesis differentiates the Israelites and their worship of a supreme invisible Creator who stands outside the manifest creation from the Mesopotamians who worshipped the sky (that 'firmament' which divides the waters on Day Two), the Canaanites who worshipped the earth (dried out on Day Three), and the Egyptians who worshipped the Sun (created on Day Four). The biblical account shows that the heavens, the sky, the earth and the sun, moon and stars are all inanimate, created entities without special divine significance, rather like the modern scientific view. This would have been a fearful blasphemy to the various nations of the ancient Near East. And this confronting account is insouciantly laid out in a page or two of mythic verses. In the context of the ancient Near East, to borrow from the language of contemporary advertising, the writer of Genesis was engaged in product differentiation in a spiritually saturated market.

We saw, at the end of the previous chapter, how the first six days of creation fall into two groups of three setting out the fixed and then the moving form of various natural phenomena. On this interpretation the pair of seventh day – the day of rest – is made up of all those who hear and follow the dictates of the wise as embodied in all that follows in the Bible.

We can also see the trajectory of seven days of creation as a rising tide of freedom of movement and autonomy where the earlier substances – light, darkness, water, sky and earth (universal, fixed and unchanging), give way to plants (living and growing but fixed in place), fish and birds and animals (living and moving but bound by their animal natures) to man (living, moving and endowed with free will).

Table 6 summarises the six days of creation as reflecting the six of the steps to freedom and happiness laid out in the *Yoga Vasishtha:*

TABLE 6: Genesis and *Yoga Vasishtha*

Step to Freedom	Day of Creation	Interpretation
Shubhech-cha Good impulse	1. Light and dark; Day and night	When a seeker of freedom encounters the teaching of the wise it is like a light turning on.
Suvicharana Propitious enquiry	2. The firmament dividing the waters above from the waters below	Water often symbolises love or desire: The light divides us and we have a desire for the higher things and also for our habitual, lower ways. This creates a need to study the teachings we have encountered and to make efforts to put them into practice to strengthen and establish the movement to the light.
Tanumanasa Refinement of the mind	3. Waters recede and dry land appears; plants	The turbulence of the mind and heart recedes somewhat, and a firmer foundation has now appeared. Also *sattva*, which is like food for further development, is more available.
Sattvapati A state of *sattva*	4. Sun, moon and stars	We now experience both the inner illumination of the clear intellect and the external guidance of the wisdom of the masters. Their light shows us a clear path in both day and night, in good times and in times of challenge
Asangsakti Insight and detachment	5. Fish and birds	We are now detached from objects of desire and aversion. Both we and they (thoughts and feelings) move freely like fish and birds moving in their proper sphere.
Padarthabhavani Non-awareness of objects	6. Animals and man	Higher reasoning which sees through the illusion of separation is available (man) but we still feel ourselves to be separate (animal).
Turiya Full realisation	7. The day of rest	We are totally free of all delusion and know ourselves to be pure consciousness with nowhere to go and nothing to do.

Genesis: The Sabbath Day

Even those of us who know almost nothing else about the Bible know that God made the world in six days and then He rested on the seventh day.

Thus the heavens and the earth were finished, and all the host of them. And on the seventh day God ended his work which he had made; and he rested on the seventh day from all his work which he had made.
And God blessed the seventh day, and sanctified it: because that in it he had rested from all his work which God created and made.[64]

Let us take a more detailed look at this Sabbath day, which is the day of rest, peace and an end to all striving – the key features of *turiya*. The description of the Sabbath Day gives us a number of clues to *turiya*. The seventh stage appears only after the heavens and the earth 'and the host of them', are finished. When all our unmanifest (heaven) and manifest (earth) tendencies and 'the host' of our strivings, our triumphs and our tragedies, our hopes and fears are all finished, the reward is complete rest. It is, as Hamlet says, a consummation devoutly to be wished. This rest comes after all the work which we have made is at an end.

And how much work do we make, for our friends and loved ones, our colleagues and acquaintances, and, of course, ourselves? Perhaps it's better we shouldn't ask! But after all the turmoil of life, all the hostages to fortune we scatter every day, all the half-baked resolutions and unkept promises, again, the reward is complete rest and peace. Not retribution, not measure for measure, not an eye for an eye. What a wonderful promise! And Jesus confirmed this principle:

Come unto me, all ye that labour and are heavy laden, and I will give you rest. Take my yoke upon you, and learn of me; for I am meek and lowly in heart: and ye shall find rest unto your souls. For my yoke is easy, and my burden is light.[65]

This is an astonishing reversal of the law of tit-for-tat of work-a-day life. This is not, of course, a prescription for irresponsibility and injustice. It speaks of an inner condition of release. If we have done harm we

---

[64] Genesis 2:1–3.
[65] Matthew 11:28–30.

should make good, but the extra part – the self-loathing, the guilt, the feelings of powerlessness, and so on – these are the works we put down and from which we enjoy rest. So we don't become a passive nonentity, coolly unavailable to those who need us – rather the opposite, in a state of freedom and peace we have much more time and energy to devote to those activities which really need doing and to which our skills are suited.

While the day of rest is not a prescription for avoiding our responsibilities, it does take us beyond the world of cause and effect. In the familiar, ordinary world we work, and we are paid; we are nice, and people are nice to us; we err, and we are punished. This tit-for-tat world is, as far as it goes, a reasonable system. It is efficient insofar as it gets us moving in approximately the right direction, because right action generally produces pleasant results and wrong action usually produces some form of kick in the rear. But it is a 'closed system' and ultimately unable to give true and lasting satisfaction and freedom. Wordsworth describes this world and the despondency it produces:

> *The world is too much with us; late and soon,*
> *Getting and spending, we lay waste our powers;*
> *Little we see in Nature that is ours;*
> *We have given our hearts away, a sordid boon!*[66]

But the Sabbath day gives us our hearts back. The promise of the Sabbath day is that we can transcend this world of reward and punishment. There is a sacredness in this state of rest after all our labour, because God blessed the seventh day, and sanctified it. The wise men and women throughout the ages experienced this realm of consciousness and bliss and they have endeavoured to lay out pathways so that we too can come to this experience of the fullness of our true Self.

And to help in this, religions have ordained formal days of rest and reflection – Friday for the Muslims, Saturday for the Jews, Sunday for the Christians. The fourth commandment, as expressed in Exodus, exhorts us to *remember* the Sabbath day, and in Deuteronomy to *keep* or *guard* the Sabbath day. In Exodus we are told to do this because on the seventh day God rested, in Deuteronomy because we were slaves in Egypt. In both cases it is not just us but our families, servants and domestic animals who

---

[66] William Wordsworth, 'The world is too much with us'.

must rest as well. It is a universal commandment for all creatures to take some rest.

In the present age formal observance of the Sabbath day is largely confined to the religiously orthodox. Even when we do manage to get some time off from work, we fill our free moments with catching up on chores and domestic tasks, or socialising, or just 'vegging out'. The last thing which occurs to us is to spend one day in seven quietly contemplating our innermost Self and applying our intelligence, faith and reason to sifting the mechanical, observable part of us from the conscious, witnessing part.

So what can we do? Hamlet tells us that the rest is silence. Perhaps, instead of a Sabbath day we could begin to infuse our lives with 'Sabbath moments' of silence, stillness and peace. **See Practices 31, 32 and 33, pages 174–175.**

By practising this regular return to a state of rest the living dream in which we find ourselves will gradually thin out and allow more and more frequent periods of complete wakefulness. Whilst most of us have worldly responsibilities which we must and should attend to, to rest, to be still and to be at peace are also a part of the divine plan. So while we are godlike in our doing and making, we are equally godlike in putting down our tools and resting from all the work which we have made.

Waking From the Dream

This deep rest in *turiya* is the fruit of the realisation that everything is woven of a single consciousness, that there is no difference between separate objects; and that the *apparent* separation is just that – an appearance only. At this level we are universal and we know no differences. The irony of *turiya* is that we have always been there and therefore don't need to strive to attain it:

> We shall not cease from exploration
> And the end of all our exploring
> Will be to arrive where we started
> And know the place for the first time.[67]

---

[67] TS Eliot, *Little Gidding IV*

How long does it take you to be you? Realising *turiya* shows us that even the seven steps to get there were illusory. The wise, knowing this unity, tell us that we were never anywhere else.

But we might say the same thing to the amnesia victim lying in hospital. They are who they are and nothing can change that. Nevertheless a process of medication, counselling and the passage of time are needed to restore their memory. Until that time the person may have flashes of remembrance, frustrating moments of disorientation, and complete failure to recall basic aspects of their real life.

We are like this amnesia victim. For us, so the wise tell us, the world we take to be real is in fact a dream. And one day we will have to wake up. In a dream in bed at night we may run from tigers or fall from buildings or achieve our heart's desire, but when we wake up all the tigers, buildings and desires are known only to have existed in our own consciousness. Even the dream 'I' disappears.

Just like waking from a night dream, or coming out of amnesia, in *turiya* we wake up from the illusion of believing ourselves to have been the dream figures of our 'waking' state: we know ourselves never to have been a doctor, lawyer, housewife or thief. We realise we needn't have worried, or become fearful, or enraged or infatuated.

Let's consider our night dreams. No matter how pleasant they are, few of us would seriously wish to lie in bed asleep for the rest of our lives without any chance of waking, just to enjoy this illusory world. Who, after all, could guarantee that all the dreams would be unendingly lovely? Do we all get to live happily ever after, even in our dreams? And who do we suppose will look after us as we lie in bed snoring away forever? Who ensures that the intravenous drip is full of nutrients and that we don't get bed sores, and who empties the bedpan?

Joining the Wise

In the waking dream world which we call reality there is a similar conundrum. While we are lost in thoughts of the past, fears of the future, self-doubt, jealously – with a little hope and a few pleasant memories, we are, essentially, asleep to the greater realms of reality and consciousness. Who is looking after us? Who looks after everyone? We spoke earlier of the words, thoughts and actions of the saints and sages continuously sending out good impulses to protect a vulnerable world and to offer guidance to those who wish to go free. By reaching the higher stages of the seven steps, and especially by going all the way to *turiya*, we join in this great act of protective service to the universe.

The wise are calling us to come out of our dream existence, and join them in their work of protecting and caring for the universe. Plato's allegory of the cave is one such call: He tells us that *we* are the prisoners in the cave chained from birth by the neck and ankles, doomed to watch the shadows on the wall of the cave, taking these shadows to be real, until we are released and compelled to stand, turn around and look at the objects of which we previously only saw the shadows. He ends the story with the freed prisoner, his eyes now seeing reality, descending into the cave to free others.

I once asked some eleven and twelve year-old children how they would like to be remembered once they had lived out their years. What would they like carved on their headstone. Many said they would like to have been of service – to cure cancer, to end war, to feed the hungry. Then one boy asked me what I'd like on my headstone. I was mildly taken aback – partly because, despite having asked the question I hadn't thought about my own answer. So I thought for a few moments and said: 'On my headstone I would like them to carve: He freed others.'[68]

This freedom involves waking out of the dream world of unreality and coming to see reality in all its glory. There is a wonderful description of this in the Book of Revelation:

> *And I saw a new heaven and a new earth: for the first heaven and the first earth were passed away … . And I John saw the holy city, new Jerusalem, coming down from God, out of heaven, prepared as a bride adorned for her husband. … and there shall be no more death, neither sorrow, nor crying, neither shall there be any more pain: for the former things are passed away. … Behold, I make all things new. … I am Alpha and Omega, the beginning and the end. … He that overcometh shall inherit all things.*[69]

Experiencing the Limitless

In *turiya* we know ourselves to be pure consciousness only, one without a second. The drama of life continues to play itself out but the knower of truth stops nowhere, and nothing stops him. We allow everything to unfold in its natural course; not elated by triumph and undisturbed by tragedy. *Turiya* is described as fullness, oneness, reality, unqualified existence and, paradoxically after all these descriptions, indescribable. In *turiya* we know ourself to be universal.

Turiya is not a state because, as we said, all other states are contained within it. It is like space. Just as the space in a room remains constant whether it is full of furniture or empty; and whether love or murder are being enacted in it. This space in the room is unaffected and contains and interpenetrates everything in that room. This space is unmoving even while objects and people circulate and move within it.

Similarly pure, limitless consciousness is the substance from which all things are made, in which they take their existence and into which they merge when their allotted span is complete. While our minds can come up with a myriad of ideas and then dismiss them, our consciousness is, ultimately, unaffected. These ideas and imaginings float in and float out but the ground of our self-consciousness remains as it has always been.

I Am What I Am

An example: at a retreat I had been particularly frustrated by the persistence of my identification with my body. Regardless of the depth of meditation, the focus of my attention or the sincerity of my efforts, I still lived inside my body, saw out of my eyes and heard through my ears. Why? How could I go free of this basic limitation?

We were studying the Chandogya Upanishad in which Narada asks Sanatkumar to teach him how to go free. Sanatkumar gives Narada a series of meditations – on speech, mind, will, and so on. And then he tells Narada that the trees, the mountains and the earth are all meditating and instructs him to 'meditate on meditation as Brahman, O Narada.'

When I heard this I immediately connected with the meditation of all these beings. Wherever I turned my attention I could feel everything was meditating – the chairs, the furniture, the flowers, and individual people at the retreat. Everything was meditating on being itself; and the mantra

---

[68] On further reflection I'd like them to add: He made it look easy.
[69] Revelation, 21:1–7.

was I AM WHAT I AM.

It was clear to me that everyone and everything was resonating with the basic knowledge that it is what it is and it is nothing other than what it is. And meditating on this as Brahman – as Absolute, limitless consciousness – took me into a world of substantial, endless, unified existence. I could turn my attention to anything or anyone and feel and understand the core of their innermost being; and more, I could feel the ocean of unbroken, unified consciousness in which all these apparently separate entities swam.

When Moses saw the bush in the desert which burnt but which was not consumed he was seeing the fire of reason and wisdom which is creative and full of knowledge and life. As he was on holy ground he was instructed to remove his shoes – the covering which separated him from universal wisdom. God told him to return to Egypt and free the enslaved Children of Israel. When Moses asked God's name, God replied I AM THAT I AM – this is the name which I heard everything meditating on.

And yet, and yet … I was still seeing out of these eyes and hearing through these ears and observing from wherever my body happened to be. Then it occurred to me – what if I turned my attention to my own body and connected with *its* meditation? I did so and I knew my body was, like everything else, meditating on being itself – a physical, human body, with all its wonderful intricacies and processes, reasonably healthy and fit for the tasks it was designed for, ready to serve and obey the dictates of the mind and heart. But no more than that – not myself, not Me, not the beginning and end of my existence. So, if I am not the body, what am I?

I put my attention on my mind. This was trickier as the mind is active (particularly mine). But I persevered and gradually I experienced the mind also meditating on just being itself: speedy, formulating thoughts, acquiring impressions, shaping them into concepts, making decisions, memories, ideas, and so on. But again, it was just itself; not me, not my mind, just a series of impressive, but largely functional mechanisms. So, if not the mind, what am I?

I put my attention on my heart, the emotional centre, and it revealed itself as a gentle flow of feeling: love, care, anxiety, hope, and so on. Just a rising and falling tide of emotion without the impact it usually has when I believe these to be *my* feelings. Again, if not my feelings, what am I?

In all of this *I* remained simply as the witnessing consciousness, unlimited by body, mind and heart. While the eyes still saw from their position in my body, I was free of this limit. I was not seeing out the eyes of others, but this ceased to be a concern because I knew myself to be free of the limits of body, mind and heart. I felt my presence to be larger and not confined to an individual body–mind–heart. I could 'flow' into the being of others and connect with them from the inside; and it was impossible to feel anything other than love, joy and understanding. There was no taint of judgment, criticism or requirement that anyone be other than who they were.

I met one lady, who is a dear friend, and I felt her intelligence, warmth, her earnestness and innocence; and also her insecurity and fear. I was not blind to the aspects of people which were troublesome or limiting; but there was no judgment or criticism.

Access to this 'state' can be gained by connecting with the meditation of any perceived object; and then shifting the perception to the body–mind–heart; and then to remain resting in awareness.

The Teaching of the Wise

Lester Levenson says there are only two types of people: those who are trying to go free consciously, and those who are trying to go free unconsciously. The former are looking for a way to go beyond mundane existence; the latter are still bedazzled by the veil of ignorance known as *maya*, and, like a thirsty person drinking sand from a mirage, they are trying to find liberation within the binding illusion, rather than finding a way to step free.

The wise, in their infinite compassion for those of us still bound by this *maya*, give us advice and guidance. Sometimes they teach, and these teachings come in all varieties (including laying out the seven steps to knowledge and freedom). Sometimes they command. The first of the Ten Commandments is 'I am' – which is then filled out: 'I am the Lord thy God which has brought thee out of the land of Egypt, out of the house of bondage. Thou shalt have no other gods before me.' Sometimes the wise trick us into enlightenment with puzzles and conundrums. The Zen masters were particularly good at this:

A student once asked Joshu: 'If I haven't anything in my mind,
*   what shall I do?'*
'Throw it out,' Joshu replied.
'But if I haven't anything, how can I throw it out?' the student replied.
'Well,' said Joshu, 'then carry it out.'

Another way in which the wise try to communicate universal wisdom is by analogy. A common analogy for the veil of illusion is that of drama. The wise tell us that all the world's a stage and all the men and women are merely players. No matter how passionately an actor throws himself into his role, when the curtain goes down and the applause dies away, he or she goes home, not as Hamlet or Portia, Iago or Lady Macbeth, but as him or herself. And when all the dreaming is over, when the shadows are left behind, when all things are made new – all the highs and lows, the misery and elation, the knowledge and ignorance, the desires and fears, the wins and losses – what then? What is left? Who are we without all this baggage born of pleasure and pain, desire and aversion? Who do *we* go home as?

Satchitananda

Our artificial and encrusted nature, woven of accumulations of desire, aversion and ignorance of our true Self, separates and isolates us from the rest of the universe. It changes and fluctuates and bends in the breeze of external events. When this artificial nature is finally dissolved and we know it to have been but a dream (or more often, a nightmare) what is left? Who are we without our fears, jealousies and ambitions? Who am I when the 'I' that I have always believed myself to be is no longer calling the shots? On those occasions when we wake up and for a few brief moments we don't know who we are or where we are – who, in fact, are we?

As usual the wise have an answer. When our false nature is extinguished our true nature is revealed; and this true nature is woven of limitless knowledge, unending consciousness and supreme bliss. It is known in Sanskrit as *satchitananda* – truth-consciousness-bliss.

When all the game playing and illusion is over we are left as limitless consciousness and our true nature – *satchitananda* – shows itself. In fact, it is always there because it is the true, ever-present nature of the universe, but we miss it because we have a mental and emotional screen which transfixes us. Like the analogy of the snake seen on a path at twilight, we feel fear and panic until a little more light shows us that the 'snake' is only a rope. We calm down and laugh at our foolishness. The question of how the snake changed into a piece of rope is meaningless. It didn't change. It was always a rope.

In the same way we were never a limited entity, identified with a body-mind-heart, subject to growth and decay and to all 'the natural shocks which flesh is heir to'. When the steps to freedom are fulfilled and we are liberated from the land of Egypt, the house of bondage, we wonder what it was that we were thinking. We know this from ordinary experience. As I said previously, if you can bear to think back on your teenage years, all the things that were a matter life and death – that special party that simply *everyone* was going to; that popular boy/girl who never looked your way; that pair of jeans you simply had to own – all now are laughably insignificant and petty. And we wonder how we could ever have taken them so seriously. If only our older wiser selves could have been there to give our younger foolish selves some really good advice. (For most of us, there were one or two people who tried to give us some guidance – they are called parents – but we know how much that helped!)

Those lost in *maya* are like those teenagers at a party, lost in a world of anticipation and self-centredness, with the music far too loud and the dangers of drink and drugs hovering nearby. The wise are there to help us go free to a world of *turiya* with its promise of a concern-free existence of limitless bliss. Our part is to heed the advice and follow it. We then experience our nature as *satchitananda* – knowledge-consciousness-bliss. We can test the truth of this assertion.

Practice 34 (page 175) is designed to help us see things without preconceptions. I try to use this practice when dealing with children, parents and colleagues. In other words I try to see them without any preconceptions or expectations. I feel a sense of surrender to them and humility in their presence and I consistently find I get real and often unexpected insight into whoever I am considering in this way. This is the limitless impersonal knowledge of *satchitananda* which leads to insight or consciousness. The sense of satisfaction and unity and 'rightness' which follows carries a taste of bliss. In *turiya* this experience of *satchitananda* is endless.

PRACTICE 30 ➤➤➤➤➤➤➤➤➤

Practise resting your attention on the centre of your body about where your navel is. Just rest there and let thoughts or considerations or expectations go. Allow the experience to deepen; if images and thoughts and feelings arise, welcome them – they are not the enemy – and let them go on their way.

As a further development of this exercise walk around with your attention on this central point in your body. Generally we live in our heads, so move the sense of 'where I am in my body' down to this central point.

PRACTICE 31 ➤➤➤➤➤➤➤➤➤

Set aside a regular part of your day for rest, peace and contemplation. Do this with meditation and other spiritual practices which appeal to you.

PRACTICE 32 ➤➤➤➤➤➤➤➤➤

Punctuate the day with frequent brief 'Sabbath moments'. Challenge yourself to pause and be still and connected to your senses frequently – try for three or four times a day and then increase the frequency.

PRACTICE 33 ➤➤➤➤➤➤➤➤➤

A rather interesting practice is known as the 'stop exercise'. (You might like to do this when no one is looking.) It is quite simple: walk easily and naturally and then just stop. The challenge is to stop on every level – physically, mentally and emotionally. Just freeze for a few moments then do it again three or four times. A surprisingly powerful exercise.

Take any object or person and rest your attention on them. Allow any preconceptions, expectations or ideas to gently pass until you are simply resting your attention on that shape or sound or whatever. If you are looking just see colour and form; if listening, just hear sound and vibration and so on. Be conscious and connected and allow the object to tell you everything you need to know about it in that moment. Don't overlay the object with 'knowledge' born of past experience.

You might gently ask: 'What do you want to teach me? What am I here to learn from you? What do you need from me? What can I give?

Allow simple knowledge to arise.

Conclusion

ester Levenson made a momentous discovery in 1952 when he was
sent home to his New York apartment to die after his second coronary. He had experienced the ups and downs of life and, as he sat in his
apartment, having been given only a few weeks to live and having been
told there was nothing more the doctors could do for him, he thought to
himself: 'Lester, you're still alive, why don't *you* try to do something about
this.' When he reflected on himself and his state he said to himself: 'Lester,
for a smart boy, you're stupid, stupid, stupid.' With all his education, work
and wealth he had not found the secret to living happily and now he was
going to die lonely, sick and depressed.

He began a process of self-enquiry into the truth and purpose of life
and he found two fundamental things: his own suppressed feelings were
the cause of all his misery and illness; and secondly, he had an innate ability to let go of these feelings.

Continuing his enquiry he found that giving love rather than receiving it
was the key to happiness; that he was happy when he was loving – either the
people he was with or the things he was doing. And he found the desire for
love and approval from others actually caused misery. So over the next few
weeks he began to let go of his desire for love and approval. And he became
happier and happier.

He was then confronted by his desire to control and change things – as
he related it, he even found himself wanting to change the end of movies.
This desire for control was the next thing he relinquished. This took him
a further few weeks. And again he found himself getting happier and
happier, more energised and healthier. He walked the streets of Manhattan
late at night just to burn off this energy.

The third step was to confront the fear of dying; the existential dread of his own extinction. So he dragged this feeling up from the depths of his subconscious and had a number of interesting insights. First, the fear of dying was not the same as dying itself; it is an ego-based defence which keeps the small self in the driver's seat, calling the shots. He let go of his fear of dying and found himself immersed in limitless bliss. Again, as he told the story, the bliss was almost uncomfortably intense. So far this journey had taken him a few months.

Finally he was walking along the street and he realised that the final barrier was none other than 'Lester Levenson' – himself as a separate ego. At that moment of realisation Lester disappeared and never came back. The rest of his story, his teaching of what he came to call the Sedona Method, and his work for the next forty-two years is readily available in books and on various websites.

I found this story and the Sedona Method inspiring and useful. More importantly this story shows that it is possible, desirable and fundamentally easy to go completely free. The only prerequisite to go free is to want to; the prerequisite to going free quickly is to want it a lot; the prerequisite to going free instantly is to want it more than anything else.

So how much do you want freedom? If you want it passionately, exclusively and with a burning desire, then this book (and others like it) can give you a few tips and the rest will take care of itself. If however your desire for freedom is not quite so incandescent then the question is how can the desire be intensified?

Lester had his coronary to get him moving; Brandon Bays had a basketball-sized tumour; Byron Katie was in a halfway house full of anger and self-hatred; Eckhardt Tolle was suicidally depressed. John Wren-Lewis was poisoned by a thief in Thailand, was nearly killed, and he woke up in a Thai hospital in a state of bliss. For all these contemporary Western figures liberation seemed to come out of the blue, as a result of trauma, seemingly unrelated to prior efforts or disciplines.

Their accounts of enlightenment and their subsequent efforts to share their knowledge and bliss are inspiring, but they all seem to have had a kick in the spiritual rear to get them over the final hurdle. Do we all need to wait for a life-and-death moment to tip us into a state of freedom? Is our attachment and identification with the things of the world including family, friends, wealth and comfort and, of course, our own individual existence, so strong that only a rude shock will awaken us?

In a way this is the question which prompted me to write this book. Can we achieve full realisation by applying the teachings of saints and sages? It is a question in my mind because after over thirty years of formal study, meditation and practical application of the teachings of the wise I can say without any doubt that I feel stronger, more focused, more centred and I move through my day with ready access to an inner core of stillness, peace and knowledge. I can fall inwardly still and tap a well-spring of knowledge in order to meet the challenges of life; I can draw on emotional resources to banish fear and agitation in myself and, to a certain extent, in others. And I can feel a deep, abiding desire for freedom and happiness with no taint of bondage or misery, for myself and others.

While I cannot say I have attained ultimate union with universal consciousness, I feel it pressing closely. And I hope this book of stories, anecdotes, knowledge and practical tips will help others attain freedom. Perhaps more quickly than I have done. After all as Lester used to say: 'How long does it take to do a three month job? How much time does it take for a person to be who they already are?'

The seven steps are a recognised series of stages accompanied by practices and activities which, if followed, will purify the being, clear the mind, settle the heart and lead to greater connection with reality.

When we attain the final stage of freedom and happiness we will recognise it from the various descriptions the wise have given us. In our progress from *shubhech-cha* to *turiya* I showed each step related to the seven days of creation. The seventh day – the day of rest – is our invitation to enter into the peace of *turiya,* universal being, one without a second.

The Characteristics of the Man of Steady Wisdom

In Chapter Two of the *Bhagavad Gita* the man of steady wisdom is described as having seven characteristics:
1. Satisfaction in the Self
2. Equanimity in pleasure and pain
3. Absence of attachment, delight and aversion
4. Complete withdrawal of senses from objects

5. Devotion to the Lord

6. Seeing the Universe as a mere dream, and finally

7. Subjugation of desire and the personal self.

This seventh characteristic, subjugation of desire and the personal self, is likened to the ocean into which all waters flow without ever altering it, filling it or causing it to break its banks. Those who treasure and hang on tenaciously to their desires for external objects cannot find ultimate peace, but all desires flow *into* those who have steady wisdom without changing them. Rather than desires flowing out towards their objects, causing agitation and instability, the desires flow in and come to rest.[70]

Similarly when the seventh chakra, coloured violet or pearly white and located at the crown of the head, is energised and in alignment we feel integrated, unified and at one with the universe. We are totally aware of the true Self, as this chakra is considered to be the point of communication between the individual and the universe.

A Review of the Seven Steps

So finally let's review these seven steps.

- At step one – *shubhech-cha* – is a desire to go free, a sense of frustration, and perhaps a glimpse into the unreality and essential futility and foolishness of merely pursuing worldly ends. We get an inkling that there are men and women who have some knowledge of how we might go free, and we either seek them out, or they may come to us by some lucky chance. We hear their teaching and respond inwardly with a feeling of assent; and we then begin to do as they recommend.

- In the second stage of *suvicharana* we do some further study of the words and teachings of the wise, making them a natural part of our make up through practice and discipline. This is true or propitious enquiry. We may find ourselves in a divided, at times turbulent, condition because the new way of living rubs up against our old habitual ways. While this may feel uncomfortable, it is in fact auspicious. It shows we are making progress. And the friction lights a sort of subtle fire in us which burns up ignorance.

[70] AM Sastry, *The Bhagavad Gita,* Samata Books, Madras, 1981, pp.79–80.

- This all leads to the third level – *tanumanasa* – where the noises in our mind cease to be such a stumbling block to reality. The mind is purified. Thoughts and feelings seem less overwhelming and the thoughts we do have are, on the whole, more useful – reminders to wake up, words and phrases of the wise and so on.

- These first three steps can repeat and repeat. We heed a good impulse, make some effort to practice, which leads to a stiller and more refined mind. But at a certain point the *sattva* or focused consciousness in our being reaches a tipping point and we enter stage four – *sattvapati*. This tipping point often shows itself as the desire to be free of pleasure as well as pain. In this state our direction towards freedom and truth is much more firmly established. Our preferences are for those things which are wholesome and pure and which assist us on our journey.

- We then enter a phase at *asangsakti* of non-attachment to passing objects and inner fancies. This freedom, inner peace and joy is the natural outcome of the previous four steps.

- *Padarthabhavani* is a condition where we see that the separation of objects and beings is illusory. We experience non-difference and the oneness of being. At this level we are aware of separate objects only if compelled to do so by circumstances or the needs of others.

- *Turiya,* the final phase, contains all the previous steps because, at this level, we know we were never anywhere else. All the yearning, striving and desire for freedom disappear. It is a transcendent state insofar as it is the experience of oneself as undifferentiated consciousness within and throughout the universe.

On this journey we experience greater and greater freedom until ultimate freedom dawns. Along the way we can turn and hold out a helping hand to those others who are also desirous of freedom. This is not an exhortation to set up a mission or embark on a crusade; if others are unwilling to move or don't even know that a movement to freedom is desirable or even possible it is unlikely that such help will be accepted. It will be seen as interference and do-gooding (at best). It is better to wait to be asked. After all everyone is entitled to choose their own path, even if that path is one of materialism and illusion, and it behoves us to respect each others' choices just as we would want our own choices to be respected.

In fact the greatest help to others is a life well lived in search of freedom. I wish you the best of good fortune with your efforts and wish you and yours all the freedom in the world.

* * * * * * *

Bibliography

Arya, Ravi Prakash (ed.) *Yoga-Vasista of Valmiki* (vol. 1-4), Parimal Publications, Delhi, 1998.

Biedermann, H (J Hulbert, trans.) *Dictionary of Symbolism: Cultural Icons and the Meanings Behind Them,* Facts on File, New York, 1992.

Bays, B, *The Journey,* HarperCollins Publishers Australia, 1999.

Bays, B, *Freedom Is: Liberating Your Boundless Potential,* New World Library, USA, 2007.

Clarke, L, *Parzival and the Stone from Heaven,* HarperCollins, London, 2001.

Csíkszentmihályi, Mihály, *Flow: The Psychology of Optimal Experience,* Harper Perennial, New York, 1991.

De Mello, A, *Awareness,* Zondervan, Michigan USA, 1990.

Gibbon, E, *The Decline and Fall of the Roman Empire,* vol. VI, Everyman, New York, 1910.

Hayward, S, *Churchill and Leadership,* Gramercy Books, New York, 2004.

Kass, L, et al. *The Beginning of Wisdom: Reading Genesis,* Simon & Schuster, 2003.

Katie, B, *Question Your Thinking, Change the World: Quotations from Byron Katie,* Hay House, 2007.

Katie, B & S Mitchell, *A Thousand Names for Joy: How to Live in Harmony with the Way Things Are,* Ebury Publishing, UK, 2007.

Katie, B & S Mitchell, *Loving What Is: Four Questions That Can Change Your Life,* Ebury Publishing, UK, 2002.

Landau, R, *God Is My Adventure,* Unwin, London, 1935.

Levenson, L, *The Power of Love,* Lawrence Crane Enterprises, USA, 2006.

Monier-Williams, M, *A Sanskrit–English Dictionary,* Oxford University Press, Oxford, 1979.

Pratchett, T, *Hogfather,* Random House, UK, 2008.

Purohit Swami, Shri, *The Geeta,* Faber & Faber, London, 1935.

Purohit Swami, Shri & WB Yeats, *The Ten Principal Upanishads,* Faber & Faber Ltd, London, 1975.

Riso, DR & R Hudson, *The Wisdom of the Enneagram*, Bantam Books, New York, 1999.

Saraswati, Shantananda, *Good Company*, Study Society, London, 1992.

Saraswati, Shantananda, *The Man Who Wanted to Meet God*, Bell Tower, New York, 1996.

Sastry, AM, *The Bhagavad Gita*, Samata Books, Madras, 1981.

Sheinkin, S, *Rabbi Harvey Rides Again*, Jewish Lights Publishing, Vermont, 2008.

Tathagatananda, S, *Journey of the Upanishads to the West*, Advaita Ashrama, Kolkata, 2002.

Thomas à Kempis (Harold Gardner SJ, ed.), *The Imitation of Christ*, Doubleday, 1955.

Tolley, D, *The Power Within: Leon MacLaren, A Memoir of his Life and Work*, BookSurge, LLC, USA, 2009.

Vimuktananda, Swami (trans.), *Aparokshanubhuti: Self Realization of Sri Shankaracharya*, Advaita Ashrama, Calcutta, 1989.

Index

A

Absolute, 133
action
    law, 12
    need, 33, 36
    real enquiry, 53, 54
    regulated by *gunas*, 130
Adi Shankara, 41–42, 125
Advaita Vedanta, 6, 37, 41
ahankara, 69, 71–72, 73, 86, 99–100
anger, 66–67
antahkarana, 86, 99
Arjuna, 8, 29, 65
art appreciation, 146
asangsakti, 124–125, 128, 132, 134, 137,
    180
attention, 12, 19, 97, 101, 102, 145, 146,
    161
awareness, 2, 4, 26, 37, 57, 73, 83, 171

B

Bays, Brandon, 101, 140, 177
Bhagavad Gita, 8, 9, 41, 44, 66, 72, 130,
    178
bliss, 7, 15, 84, 96, 144, 166, 172–173,
    177
Brahman, 128, 170
Brahmananda, 40, 41
Buddha, 66–67, 157
buddhi, 91–94
Buddhism, 41
Bunyan, John, 30

C

causal form, 148–150
chakras, 9, 40, 44, 179
Chandogya Upanishad, 55, 169

chitta, 94–95, 98
choice, 137
Christian tradition, 40, 85, 96, 166
Colet, John, 46
consciousness
    higher, 44, 59, 66, 116
    limitless, 84, 133, 161
    qualities, 104–105
    raising, 4, 11
    satchitananda, 173
    unifying, 124, 125, 144
    universal, 19, 95, 128, 151, 167, 169
    will of the Absolute, 133
conviction
    regulated by *gunas*, 130
Creation, seven days — *see* Genesis
creative intelligence, 93
circles of mankind, 10, 11, 44–46,
    117–119, 120
Csíkszentmihályi, Mihály, 147–148

D

detachment, 18, 97, 124–125, 137
discipline, 9, 12, 13, 79, 149, 154, 156,
    160, 179
discursive mind, 86–87
dream existence, 7, 166–168
dreams, 79, 81, 84, 89, 98

E

ego
    ahankara, 69–70, 73, 99–100
    barrier to freedom, 16–18
enlightenment, 21, 22, 108, 119, 126,
    162, 177
enquiry
    propitious, 49, 52, 54, 179
    real or true, 54–55, 56, 64, 73

ABOUT GILBERT S. MANE

Gilbert S. Mane is a writer, keynote speaker and educational consultant. He started his working life as a lawyer. After a decade of that he jumped at the offer of becoming Headmaster of John Colet School in Sydney. He did that for twenty-six years. He now enjoys writing and speaking, and helping other school principals and staff. He also gets in as much ballroom dancing as he can. About being a lawyer? Better you don't ask! He lives (and dances) happily in Sydney, Australia with his wife.

Author's note to this reprint:

Subsequent to writing this book my spiritual path took me away from membership of the Sydney School of Practical Philosophy. That step in no way diminishes the love, admiration and debt of profound gratitude that I feel towards that organisation and the many wonderful people who have remained its students.

www.gilbertmane.com

NOTES

Printed in Dunstable, United Kingdom

71491339R00117